# Where to See
# **Wildlife**
# on Vancouver
# Island

# Where to See
# **Wildlife**
# on Vancouver
# Island

*by*

## Kim Goldberg

# HARBOUR PUBLISHING
Madeira Park and Vancouver, BC 1997

**Harbour Publishing**
P.O. Box 219
Madeira Park, BC
VON 2H0 Canada

Cover, maps, page design and composition
by Martin Nichols, Lionheart Graphics.
Cover photos: Killer Whale and Brant, Frank Stoney; Marbled Murrelet, Mark Hobson; Blood Star, Katherine Ikona; Cougar, BC Environment; Pacific Tree Frog, Jay Patterson; Northern (Steller's) Sea Lions, Trudy Chatwin; author photo, Shirley Goldberg.

Printed and bound in Canada.

The author gratefully acknowledges the financial assistance of the Wildlife Program, Vancouver Island Region, of the BC Ministry of Environment, Lands and Parks for providing funding toward her work on this book.

**Canadian Cataloguing in Publication Data**

Goldberg, Kim, 1954-
    Where to see wildlife on Vancouver Island

    Includes index.
    ISBN 1-55017-160-7

    1. Wildlife viewing sites—British Columbia—Vancouver Island—
Guidebooks. 2. Vancouver Island (B.C.)—Guidebooks.
I.Title.
QL221.B7G64 1997    591.9711    C97-910120-4

# Contents

# Acknowledgements

Many people have contributed to this book by generously sharing their knowledge and research with me, answering my numerous questions and, in many instances, providing feedback and corrections on portions of the manuscript. Any errors that persisted to the final draft are mine alone. My thanks to: Matt Austin, Steve Baillie, Betty Brooks, Kim Brunt, Melda Buchanan, Syd Cannings, Don Cecile, Trudy Chatwin, Tim Clermont, Bruce Cousens, Jim Darling, Neil Dawe, Mike Delaronde, Adrian Dorst, Graeme Ellis, David Ewart, Debby Funk, Larry Goldberg, Thor Henrich, Rick Ikona, Annemarie Koch, Charlene Lee, Janis Leach, Tim Lomas, Andy MacKinnon, Derrick Marven, Rick McKelvey, Bill Merilees, Alison Mewett, David Nagorsen, Karen Morrison, Terry Morrison, Peter Olesiuk, Jeanie Paterson, Jay Patterson, Leah Ramsay, George Reid, Hans Roemer, Ann Scarfe, Keith Taylor, Bryon Thompson, Bob Waldon, Bruce Whittington, and everyone else who communicated with me about this project.

It would not have been possible for me to write this book without funding from the Wildlife Program, Vancouver Island Region, of the BC Ministry of Environment, Lands and Parks. I would like to extend special thanks to my Ministry advisory team consisting of Doug Janz, Rick Davies and Elizabeth Stanlake from Wildlife Branch, and Rik Simmons from BC Parks. They worked with me from the outset of this project, helping determine which sites to include, tracking down documents and other information, and vetting my manuscript. Ms. Stanlake, the Ministry's Wildlife Viewing and Planning Coordinator, also served as technical editor on the manuscript, improving it considerably. David Fraser from Wildlife Branch provided valuable assistance and natural history expertise by supplying further information and corrections to the manuscript and photo captions.

This book would be much the poorer without the more than 200 colour photographs illustrating many of the diverse animals, plants and habitats on Vancouver Island. My thanks to Frank Stoney, Don Cecile, Katherine and Rick Ikona, David Fraser, Steve Baillie, Trudy Chatwin, Jay Patterson, Shirley Goldberg, Mark Hobson, Jim Darling, Graeme Fowler, David Nagorsen, Leah Ramsay, Christian Engelstoft, Cris Guppy, Ian Lane, Richard Beard and Lothar Kirchner for contributing slides to the book, greatly enhancing its usefulness.

Keith Taylor kindly allowed me to include his excellent bird checklist for Vancouver Island. I am similarly grateful to Cris Guppy, Steve Ansell and Richard Beard for supplying materials for the butterfly appendix. I thank the people at Harbour Publishing for doing a great job of putting it all together and for being enthusiastic about this book from the outset. And last but never least, I thank my mother Shirley Goldberg for dutifully recording mileages and directions on our excursions, for carrying the "cougar stick" on the trails, and for instilling a deep appreciation of nature and the outdoors in me at an early age.

# Island Wildlife Viewing Specialties

**Birdwatching** Located along the busy Pacific Flyway for migratory birds, Vancouver Island has dozens of choice locales for birdwatchers—including most sites in this guide. See page 153 for a checklist showing seasonal abundance of 387 bird species recorded on the island. A few sites and events of special interest to birdwatchers are the fall raptor migration at **East Sooke Park** (30), shorebird migrations at **Tofino Flats** (86), spring Brant migration and festival at **Parksville/Qualicum Beach** (92) and the Trumpeter Swan Festival at **Courtenay River Estuary** (100).

**Whale Watching** People come from all over the world to watch whales on both coasts of Vancouver Island. **Long Beach** on the west coast (82) offers seasonal viewing of Gray Whales, and **Johnstone Strait & Blackfish Sound** on the east coast (134) is one of the world's best places to see Killer Whales.

**Sea Lions and Seabird Viewing** The Strait of Georgia is churning with more than two thousand sea lions and tens of thousands of seabirds each November to March during the arrival and spawning of Pacific Herring. Good vantage points include **Northumberland Channel** (58), **Deep Bay & Baynes Sound** (96) and Lambert Channel en route to **Helliwell Provincial Park** (98).

**Salmon Viewing** Every year, wild salmon return to spawn in the Vancouver Island waterways where they were born. Good spots to observe this impressive spectacle are **Goldstream Provincial Park** (44), **Stamp Falls Provincial Park** (76), **Big Qualicum Hatchery** (94) and **Elk Falls Provincial Park** (118).

**Tidepool Viewing** Vancouver Island's shoreline offers great opportunities for close-up viewing of intertidal creatures. Check out **Botanical Beach Provincial Park** (34), **Whiffen Spit** (32) and **Nanaimo Waterfront Promenade** (60).

**Watching Bears and other Large Land Mammals**
Cougar, Gray Wolf, Black Bear, Roosevelt Elk and Black-tailed Deer inhabit much of Vancouver Island. Read the Bear and Cougar Precautions (20), then visit these sites: **Green Mountain** (54), **Strathcona Provincial Park—Elk River Valley** and **Thelwood Creek** (120, 122), **Menzies Elk Demonstration Forest** (124) and the **Sayward to Port McNeill Highway** (132).

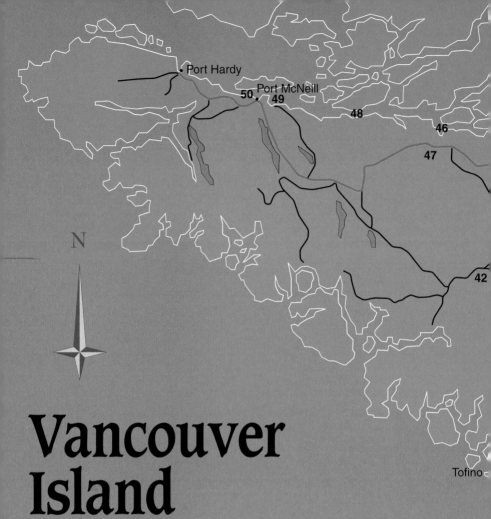

Port Hardy

Port McNeill

50. 49

48

46

47

42

N

Tofino

# Vancouver Island

It's small wonder that 387 bird species have been recorded on Vancouver Island, and Victoria has been dubbed the "bird finding capital of Canada" by more than a few keen birders. Vancouver Island's proliferation of whale watching and wildlife watching boat charters attests to the reliable presence of whales, seals, sea lions, porpoises and dolphins in the surrounding waters.

Vancouver Island supports 25 percent of the world's Trumpeter Swan population each winter, 100 percent of the world's endangered Vancouver Island Marmots, and receives an annual "sail past" of 21,000 Gray Whales each spring.

Wildlife watching is so popular on Vancouver Island, and the opportunities so abundant, that several communities host annual wildlife festivals featuring their "trademark" animal. These include the Brant Festival in Parksville/Qualicum Beach each April, the Trumpeter Swan Festival in Courtenay/Comox each February, the Pacific Rim Whale Festival in Ucluelet and Tofino each March and April, the Sea Lion Festival in Nanaimo each January (cancelled in 1997, but may resume in the future), and the Great Blue Heron Festival in Duncan each October.

The diversity of wildlife on Vancouver Island is matched by the diversity of vegetation and habitat. You'll find lush, mossy rain forests on the island's west coast where magnificent Western Redcedar trees are 1,000 years old and receive more than 300 centimetres (120 inches) of rain annually. A mountainous backbone runs down the centre of the island with the tallest peaks rising above 2,000 metres (6,500 feet).

Fertile lowlands, productive estuaries and Douglas-fir forests dominate Vancouver Island's east side, which contains astounding pockets of near-desert habitat in the rainshadow belt on the island's southeast coast and on some of the Gulf Islands. These are so arid that Brittle Prickly-pear Cactus grows there! Vancouver Island's mild climate and excellent system of roads and parks allow comfortable, year-round viewing and access to many exceptional wildlife sites, yielding experiences and memories that are sure to last a lifetime.

The 50 sites selected in this book are known for high-quality wildlife viewing, and they all offer a good probability of seeing something on any visit. Almost all are readily accessible by vehicle and/or ferry. Most of the sites have an established trail system, and many also have interpretive materials to aid you in your quest to observe and identify wild creatures in their natural habitat. No pristine wilderness areas have been included, not just because of their inaccessibility, but because wildlife viewing is not always compatible with wildlife protection, even when viewers conscientiously adhere to the wildlife viewing ethics on page 18. Human presence, particularly if it is constant and high volume, can interfere with feeding, mating, nest-tending, loafing and other activities essential to wild animals, or it can degrade their habitat. It is indeed possible to "love nature to death." However, the public's increasing interest in wildlife and nature also benefits wild creatures by placing a higher priority on protecting critical habitat, enforcing anti-poaching laws and safeguarding vulnerable and endangered species.

*Gulls gathered at north end of Denman Island during herring spawn.*
*Photo:Trudy Chatwin*

Wild animals and our opportunities to view them do not exist in a vacuum. They are very much affected by societal and natural forces at work. As of October 1996, 65 species or subspecies of vertebrate animals in British Columbia, and 224 vascular plants, were on the provincial government's Red List of species that are threatened or endangered or candidates for these designations. Some of those species are described and illustrated in this book, such as the Vancouver Island Marmot and Marbled Murrelet.

Natural factors such as weather and predation are sometimes responsible for a species' decline. But these days, the more common reason is habitat loss or degradation due to development, industrial activity, recreational use and urbanization. The ongoing industrial practice of clearcut logging on Vancouver Island, and the related pulp mill activity along Georgia Strait, place tremendous pressure on wildlife and habitat, and are frequently at odds with the island's other two principal industries: tourism and commercial fishing. Salmon spawning streams continue to be damaged and destroyed by logging activity, despite tougher governmental regulations on the industry.

The Marbled Murrelet, which nests in old-growth forest, was Red-Listed in BC in 1996 due to continued loss of nesting habitat from logging.

Similarly, real estate development and people's desire for "water view" property are no blessing for the numerous estuaries along Vancouver Island's increasingly populated east coast. Estuaries are places where rivers flow into the sea. They are extremely sensitive and biologically productive marine ecosystems, supporting huge numbers of birds, fish and intertidal creatures. Although British

Columbia's estuaries comprise less than 3 percent of the province's shoreline, they are used by 80 percent of all coastal wildlife, and they support Canada's largest wintering population of waterbirds. Sadly, estuaries are also the most imperiled of BC's ecosystems. At least two estuaries listed in this book, Englishman River and Cluxewe River, have lost the sandspit portion of their ecosystem to RV parks. Many other estuaries on eastern Vancouver Island have some form of development or industrial activity on or near them. Fortunately, agencies such as The Nature Trust of British Columbia exist to purchase critical habitat, thereby ensuring its future. Many of the estuaries and wetlands listed in this book are now Nature Trust properties.

## Highways

While I was researching and writing this book in 1996, various parts of the Vancouver Island highway system were undergoing, or slated for, a substantial realignment involving a new Inland Highway that will eventually extend from Parksville to Campbell River, as well as a bypass around Nanaimo and various alterations elsewhere. Most of these new routes, which may be the principal traffic corridors by the time you read this, were not completed during my research. The new Inland Highway, which was open from Parksville to Mud Bay in fall 1996, is now called Highway 19. And the "old" Island Highway, formerly called Highway 19 along that stretch of coast, is now 19A. The new Inland Highway is scheduled to be completed up to Courtenay by the end of 1998, and to Campbell River by 2002, with the corresponding sections of the old, coastal highway being renumbered from 19 to 19A.

My mileages and directions in this book are all taken from the old, coastal Island Highway, which runs through most of the communities mentioned. To avoid confusion over highway numbers, I often refer to the "old" Island Highway as the "coast highway." I hope this situation doesn't send you off on a wild goose chase, since that's probably not the type of wildlife viewing you had in mind! If you are unfamiliar with Vancouver Island, you will want to travel with a good, up-to-date road map.

Look for the blue and white Wildlife Watch symbol on road signs. It signals a viewing site that is part of a constantly expanding network of wildlife viewing opportunities throughout BC. British Columbia Wildlife Watch is a program designed to protect and promote wildlife viewing opportunities. It encourages public understanding and appreciation of fish, wildlife and habitat.

## The Metric System

Canada uses the metric system of weights and measures.

Distances in this book are given in kilometres, and area in hectares. To convert from kilometres to miles, multiply by 0.62. To convert from hectares to acres, multiply by 2.5.

## Names

To make the book as useful as possible, all common names that refer to a single species are capitalized (e.g., Killer Whale, Great Blue Heron, Western Redcedar), while generic names that refer to two or more species are not (e.g., whales, herons, cedars). This lets you know whether an animal or plant mentioned for a site has been identified down to the species level. But we're not out of the woods yet! As anyone with even a passing interest in botany, birdwatching, or other aspects of natural history knows, one species can have several common names. Species also undergo name changes periodically as scientists re-evaluate their taxonomic status. Common names used in this book conform to those used by the provincial government and the Royal British Columbia Museum at the time of publication. The corresponding Latin names for any species listed in this book can be found in the following handbooks: *Plants of Coastal British Columbia, Mammals of British Columbia, Reptiles of British Columbia, Amphibians of British Columbia, National Geographic Society's Field Guide to the Birds of North America, Coastal Fishes of the Pacific Northwest, National Audubon Society Field Guide to North American Butterflies, National Audubon Society Field Guide to North American Seashore Creatures.*

## And finally...

Don't get discouraged if you visit some of these sites without seeing the species mentioned here. The thrill, magic and challenge of wildlife viewing springs from its unpredictability. You simply never know what might be around that next bend in the trail. Take that away, and what you have is a zoo-viewing experience. With the exception of a few specific wildlife events such as the spring Brant assembly at Parksville/Qualicum Beach or the winter Chum run at Goldstream

*Spotting scopes or binoculars are mandatory for serious wildlife watchers.*
*Photo: Kim Goldberg*

Provincial Park, nature doesn't offer bankable guarantees on being able to drive somewhere, plant your feet on the ground, stare straight ahead, and witness a particular animal—or any animals!

You will have more clues about good wildlife viewing opportunities as you become familiar with nature's annual cycles on Vancouver Island. Stately Bald Eagles, seen year-round along our coastline, are drawn to rivers and estuaries in the fall (September to December) when salmon return to spawn. Rufous Hummingbirds return to the island each spring (late March, early April), coinciding with the blooming of Red-flowering Currant and Salmonberry. Thousands of sea ducks, gulls and sea lions descend on Georgia Strait each winter for a wild and boisterous feeding frenzy on vast schools of Pacific Herring that arrive in December and spawn in late February and early March.

For best wildlife viewing, you must be patient, keen-eyed and aware of your surroundings. What's above you? At your feet? Under that log? Rustling in the grass? A good pair of binoculars will certainly boost your chances of seeing something. And field guidebooks, local checklists or other interpretive materials for a site will help you figure out what it is. Checklists and brochures are often available from park nature houses, tourist bureaus or local naturalist clubs. The Field Naturalist store in downtown Victoria, on the corner of Blanshard and View, stocks the biggest selection of field guides and checklists on Vancouver Island (phone: 250-388-4174). The Victoria Rare Bird Alert (phone: 250-592-3381) is also useful.

North of Victoria, your best bet is the Backyard Wildbird and Nature Store in Nanaimo (phone: 250-390-1633) or Nanaimo's Rare Bird Alert (phone: 250-390-3029). But ultimately, in the exhilarating game of chance called wildlife viewing, you must simply take each sighting for the gift it is and let nature withhold the rest of her mysteries and wonders for future encounters. Enjoy!

*Kim Goldberg*
*goldberg@freenet.carleton.ca*
*Nanaimo, British Columbia*

# Wildlife Viewing Ethics

supplied by
British Columbia Wildlife Watch

 I t may seem odd to think that animals can be "watched to death," but overuse of wilderness areas and harassment by humans can harm wildlife. Always follow this code of conservation ethics when viewing wildlife:

- **Keep all vehicles on designated roads.**
  Vehicles that wander off roads can destroy vegetation.

- **Keep to marked trails.**
  Using trails protects plant life and assists animals in adapting to human movement.

- **Be considerate of wildlife.**
  Stress is harmful to animals. Use binoculars to view them from a distance rather than approach them closely. Never chase or flush animals from cover. Always respect their nests and dens.

- **Be considerate of others.**
  Respect the space of others who are viewing wildlife in the same area as you.

- **Control pets.**
  Pets are a hindrance to wildlife viewing. They may chase, injure or kill wild animals. Leave pets at home or keep them under control.

- **Keep British Columbia clean.**
  Leave the environment unchanged by your visit. Place garbage in receptacles, where provided, or take your garbage with you.

■ **Take only the right souvenirs.**
Take home memories and photographs. Leave flowers, plants, rocks, fossils, artifacts, shells and woods as you find them. Never touch or feed wild animals. Baby animals are seldom abandoned or orphaned, and it's against the law to take them away.

■ **Report environmental abuse.**
If you see others abusing the environment or bothering animals, report their vehicle licence numbers to local authorities or the nearest conservation officer.

*Use spotting scopes and binoculars to view from a distance. Photo: Kim Goldberg*

# Bear and Cougar Precautions

Black Bears and Cougars can potentially be encountered almost anywhere on Vancouver Island. Just ask the people who found a Cougar roaming the underground parkade of the Empress Hotel in downtown Victoria! Fortunately, large predators will generally avoid humans if given the chance. Exciting as it may be to view one of these magnificent creatures up close, this event can also be dangerous. You should never do anything to intentionally attract a bear or Cougar or lure one closer for a picture. Bears are readily attracted to human food and garbage. Cougars, if hungry enough, can be attracted to the rapid movements and high-pitched sounds of pets and small children, which they may perceive as prey.

Strategies for avoiding a bear or Cougar encounter are similar for the two animals. But strategies for reacting to an attack differ due to the fact that a Black Bear (the only bear species on Vancouver Island) is usually attacking for a different reason than a Cougar. If a Black Bear charges you, it has probably been surprised and may be protecting cubs or a food source. The bear may rush you and veer off at the last minute. Your best strategy is to be as calm and non-threatening as possible. If a Cougar attacks you, it is probably looking for a meal, in which case you want to make yourself appear as large and aggressive and difficult to eat as possible. However, there are no absolute rules when encountering a bear or Cougar. You must use your own judgment to assess the situation, determine the animal's intent and select your response. There have been "predatory" Black Bear attacks in which the bear was out for a meal when it attacked a human.

## TO AVOID A BEAR OR COUGAR ENCOUNTER

- Hike in groups of two or more people.
- Make noise as you hike by talking, singing, whistling, clapping, calling out or wearing a bell.
- Don't let dogs and small children run ahead on the trail.
- Watch for bear or Cougar tracks or droppings.
- Read all cautionary signs about recent bear or Cougar sightings posted at trailheads.
- Be especially alert for bears near berry patches and salmon spawning areas.
- Walk with a large stick (useful in a Cougar encounter).
- Don't store food in your tent.
- Don't sleep in the same clothes you cook in.
- Stay away from dead animals.

## IF YOU ENCOUNTER A BLACK BEAR:

- Don't run or turn your back.
- Remain calm and back away slowly, speaking in a gentle, steady voice.
- Do nothing to excite the bear.
- Avoid eye contact.

## IF A BEAR CHARGES YOU:

- Drop a daypack or other object to distract it.
- Abandon any food.
- Try to retreat, seeking shelter in a car or building if possible. Trees are not advisable, as Black Bears are agile climbers.
- If the bear is about to make contact, drop to the ground and "play dead." If the attack persists for more than a few seconds, fight back vigorously using fists, rocks, sticks or anything you can.

## IF YOU ENCOUNTER A COUGAR:

- Pick up small children or pets immediately.
- Give the Cougar an escape route.
- Back away slowly, talking in a loud, threatening voice.
- Enlarge yourself by raising arms or large sticks.
- Do not turn your back, run or crouch down.
- Maintain eye contact.

## IF A COUGAR ATTACKS YOU:

- Fight back immediately any way you can and as vigorously as you can, using rocks, sticks, fists, feet, fishing poles or whatever you can grab. Many people have survived Cougar attacks this way. Unlike most Black Bears, if a Cougar attacks you it is probably looking for a meal. You must show it you are not easy prey.

# Calendar of Vancouver Island Wildlife Events

## January

- Sea Lion Festival held at Harmac Pulp Mill in Nanaimo. Cancelled in 1997, but may resume in future years. (p. 58)
- Bald Eagles reach peak numbers at Goldstream Park. (p. 44)

## February

- Trumpeter Swan Festival held in Courtenay, first week of February. (p. 100)

## March

- Pacific Rim Whale Festival held in Ucluelet and Tofino in last two weeks of March and first week of April, celebrating the northward migration of 21,000 Gray Whales along Vancouver Island's west coast. (p. 82)

## April

- Brant Festival held in Parksville and Qualicum Beach in early April, celebrating the migratory stopover of 20,000 Brant geese. (p. 92)

## May

- Up to 10,000 Bonaparte's Gulls congregate in Active Pass. (p. 42)

## June

- Very low tides during daylight hours permit good tidepool viewing in intertidal zones.

## July

- Killer Whales reach peak numbers in Johnstone Strait and Blackfish Sound in July and August as they pursue salmon and other fish passing through these waters. (p. 134)

## August

- Several hundred Wood Ducks gather on the Duncan sewage lagoons from late summer into early fall. (p. 50)

## September

- Hawk Watch occurs in East Sooke Regional Park on the third or fourth Sunday in September, where you can observe hundreds of Turkey Vultures, along with hawks and eagles, crossing the Juan de Fuca Strait on the warm air thermals rising off the steep bluffs. (p. 30)

## October

- Chum run at Goldstream Provincial Park begins in the third week of October and continues through late December, offering excellent opportunities to view salmon spawning. (p. 44)

- Underwater viewing room at Big Qualicum Hatchery offers best viewing of Chum, Coho and Chinook Salmon from October to December. (p. 94)

## November

- Thousands of Trumpeter Swans arrive at Vancouver Island estuaries and wetlands and remain until March. (pp. 38, 48, 52, 56, 70, 78, 82, 100, 108, 122, 130, 132, 138)

- More than 2,000 Northern and California Sea Lions descend on Georgia Strait in anticipation of the December arrival and March spawning of vast schools of Pacific Herring. (pp. 42, 44, 58, 68, 80, 82, 92, 96, 98, 114, 126, 134)

## December

- Southbound Gray Whales, en route to Mexican calving lagoons, pass by Long Beach (p. 82) and Botanical Beach and French Beach. (p. 34)

- Naturalist clubs in each community hold their annual Christmas Bird Count, where both expert and amateur birdwatchers are needed.

*Great Blue Heron. Photo: Katherine Ikona*

# 50 WILDLIFE VIEWING SITES

East Sooke. Photo: Kim Goldberg

# SECTION 1
# South Island

# Victoria Waterfront

*Ocean vistas, shorebirds and seabirds*

*Black Oystercatcher. Photo: Trudy Chatwin*

This scenic waterfront drive, forming part of the Victoria Harbour Bird Sanctuary, offers excellent opportunities to view numerous ducks, gulls, shorebirds and occasionally marine mammals plus spectacular ocean vistas as you wend your way through some of Victoria's most exclusive neighbourhoods. Beginning at the corner of Douglas Street and Dallas Road on the edge of Beacon Hill Park, proceed east along Dallas Road to Clover Point. The city's sewage outfall makes this a prime location to get your gulls sorted out if you're up to the challenge. With seven regularly occurring species in Victoria (and at least another nine recorded), and with the variety of summer, winter and immature plumages for each, after a few studious sessions at Clover Point you will never call them "just sea gulls" again. The adult **Heermann's Gull**, which you're likely to see on the rocks in late summer, is unmistakable with its white head and red bill.

In spring and summer look for rafts of **Rhinoceros Auklet** (so named for the yellowish horn at the base of its bill) feeding offshore. If you're especially lucky and keen-eyed, you may see a rare **Tufted Puffin** amidst the "rhinos" in late June or early July. In September and early October, when you hear **Common Terns** screaming overhead, you'll probably find a **Parasitic Jaeger**, a predatory seabird, chasing a tern and forcing it to disgorge its fish dinner which the jaeger captures in mid-air. In any season, expect to see **Black Oystercatchers** on the rocks and resident **Harlequin Ducks** around the shore.

**DIRECTIONS:** *From downtown Victoria, drive south on Douglas Street to its terminus on Dallas Road. Turn left and proceed along the waterfront, choosing the streets that keep you closest to the water.*

VICTORIA WATERFRONT DRIVE

Arbutus

Hillside

Beach

N

Cook

Douglas

Dallas

Hollywood

Victoria Harbour

STRAIT OF JUAN DE FUCA

Continue your waterfront drive to Oak Bay, which is home to some 5,000 water-birds in winter including **Pied-billed Grebe**, **Hooded Merganser** and **American Wigeon**. In April–May and August–November, look for flocks of migrating **Bonaparte's Gulls** (small with black head in breeding plumage) feeding along the beach. In summer, you are likely to see **Pelagic Cormorants** and **Pigeon Guillemots** in the bay, since they are nesting just offshore on the Chain Islets. Nearby Discovery Island is a pupping area for **Harbor Seals**, which can be seen any-where along the waterfront throughout the year.

Proceed to Cattle Point (11 km from the start of this tour), where you'll have a good opportunity to view **Marbled Murrelets** nearly year-

*Harlequin Ducks. Photo: Frank Stoney*

round, although the best viewing location is farther along the drive at Cadboro Point and Ten Mile Point where the headland places you closer to their flight path. This tiny seabird has garnered much publicity in recent years because of its dependence on old-growth forest for nesting. Due to continued habitat loss from logging, the Marbled Murrelet was placed on BC's Red List of threatened and endangered species in 1996.

*Pelagic species such as this Northern Fulmar (left) and Tufted Puffin (above), usually found far offshore, are occasionally spotted from Clover Point.*
*Fulmar photo: Frank Stoney*
*Puffin photo: Trudy Chatwin*

# East Sooke Regional Park

*Rugged terrain noted for raptors*

*Turkey Vulture. Photo: D.F. Fraser*

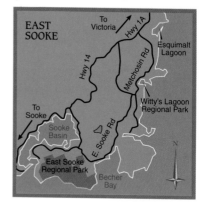

Photo: Shirley Goldberg

For a rugged, west coast day hike that takes you through lush rain forest, along windswept bluffs and down to the ocean's edge, you can't do better than the 10-kilometre Coast Trail in East Sooke Park, just a one-hour drive from Victoria. The park's claim to fame among wildlife watchers is the fact that it is one of the best sites in the Pacific Northwest to observe fall raptor migration. For four weeks beginning in mid-September, up to one thousand **Turkey Vultures** exploit the mid-day thermals (warm air currents) rising from the bluffs to carry them across the 20-kilometre narrows of Juan de Fuca Strait to their winter range in California and farther south. On a good day (warm and sunny with light north winds), you may see hundreds in the sky spiraling upward in a funnel-shaped "kettle," revealing the contours of the thermal. A kettle will often contain more than one species, with Turkey Vultures being at the top since they are the best gliders.

Also making the southbound crossing to the Olympic Peninsula in Washington state are significant numbers of **Sharp-shinned** and **Red-tailed Hawks**, and lesser numbers of **Osprey**, **Bald Eagles**, **Northern Harriers**, **Cooper's Hawks**, **American Kestrels**, **Merlins**, **Peregrine Falcons**, **Northern Goshawks** and **Rough-legged Hawks** (early October). Even one or two **Broad-winged Hawks**

**DIRECTIONS:** *From Victoria, drive to Colwood via Highway 1A, then proceed toward Sooke on Highway 14. For the Witty's Lagoon detour, turn left onto Metchosin Road 2.5 km beyond the Goldstream Avenue junction in Colwood. Proceed 9.5 km to marked park entrance on left (or get on Metchosin Road from Lagoon Road if you are coming from Esquimalt Lagoon). 1.2 km beyond Witty's Lagoon, turn right onto Happy Valley Road, then left onto Rocky Point Road. After 14 km on Rocky Point Road (which becomes East Sooke Road), you will arrive at the Becher Bay Road entrance (Aylard Farm) to East Sooke Park.*

are spotted each year, to the great excitement of local birdwatchers since this hawk is rarely seen west of Alberta. The fall hawk migration is also a good opportunity to see **Golden Eagles**, the all-brown cousin to our more familiar Bald Eagle. Under good conditions you may spot a dozen riding the thermals, which are at their best from 10:30 a.m. to 1:00 p.m.

Your best vantage point is the Beechey Head look-out, a 40-minute trek through the woods beginning at the top of the Aylard Farm parking lot (Becher Bay Road entrance). The look-out puts you quite close to the birds, but if it's fogged in you'll do better on the grassy fields near the parking lot. Phone Capital Regional District Parks to find out the date for the one-day Hawk Watch (usually the third or fourth Sunday in September) when park

*Red-tailed Hawk. Photo: Steve Baillie*

naturalists are on hand with displays and spotting scopes. If you go on another day, pick the first day of good weather after several days of bad. The hawks and

vultures are grounded on this side during bad weather. On your drive out to East Sooke you can stop at two other choice birdwatching sites in the region: Esquimalt Lagoon (from Highway 1A follow the signs to Fort Rodd Hill National Historic Site and drive across the spit enclosing the lagoon) and Witty's Lagoon Regional Park off Metchosin Road.

*Look for the distinctive pink (when backlit) tail of the Red-tailed Hawk. Photo: BC Environment*

| | |
|---|---|
| **Capital Regional District Parks:** | 250-478-3344 |
| **Recorded Information:** | 250-474-PARK |
| **World Wide Web:** | http://vvv.com/crd/ |
| | parkhome.html |

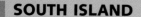

# Whiffen Spit

*Photo: Kim Goldberg*

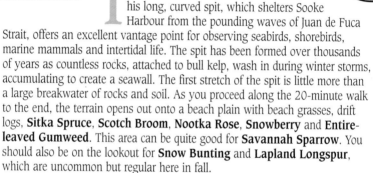

*Natural seawall rich with shore life*

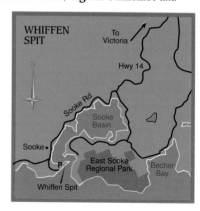

*Heermann's Gull. Photo: Rick Ikona*

This long, curved spit, which shelters Sooke Harbour from the pounding waves of Juan de Fuca Strait, offers an excellent vantage point for observing seabirds, shorebirds, marine mammals and intertidal life. The spit has been formed over thousands of years as countless rocks, attached to bull kelp, wash in during winter storms, accumulating to create a seawall. The first stretch of the spit is little more than a large breakwater of rocks and soil. As you proceed along the 20-minute walk to the end, the terrain opens out onto a beach plain with beach grasses, drift logs, **Sitka Spruce**, **Scotch Broom**, **Nootka Rose**, **Snowberry** and **Entire-leaved Gumweed**. This area can be quite good for **Savannah Sparrow**. You should also be on the lookout for **Snow Bunting** and **Lapland Longspur**, which are uncommon but regular here in fall.

Most of the seabirds and shorebirds are on the ocean side of the spit, from which you can gaze across the water to the snow-capped mountains on the Olympic Peninsula in Washington state. **Heermann's Gulls** are numerous in late summer and fall near the shore. You should also see the much smaller **Bonaparte's Gull** among them. **Western Gull** can sometimes be seen from August or early September through winter. Look for **Marbled Murrelet**, **Pigeon Guillemot** and **Common Murre** offshore. Among the shorebirds, **Black Turnstones** are common all along the ocean side, and **Black Oystercatchers** like to probe the beach along the far end of the spit. In late summer and fall, look for **Western** and **Least Sandpipers**, **Greater** and **Lesser Yellowlegs**, and **Short-billed** and

**DIRECTIONS:** *Whiffen Spit Road is 1 km beyond downtown Sooke (37 km west of Victoria) on Highway 14. Parking lot is at end.*

*Blood Star, also called Pacific Henricia.*
*Photo: Katherine Ikona*

Long-billed Dowitchers. **Harbor Seals** are common year-round, and **Killer Whale** sightings are possible on the ocean side.

The rocky beach on the ocean side is worth exploring at low tide. Intertidal creatures found here include **Sea Lemon** (one of the largest nudibranchs on the west coast, reaching lengths of 25 centimetres) plus two other nudibranchs: **Monterey Doris** and **Ringed Doris**. **Leathery Anemone** is buried in the gravel near the low-tide line. **Bushy-headed Peanut Worm** and **Agassiz's Peanut Worm** are under the rocks. Be sure to replace any stones you move in your search. Various crabs and limpets are also present. Always be aware of the tides when you explore Whiffen Spit so you don't get stranded. The base of the spit (near the parking lot) is sometimes breached at high tides.

*Black Scoters, the least common of the three scoter species, are regularly seen here.*
*Photo: Don Cecile*

# Botanical Beach Provincial Park

*Photo: L.R. Ramsay*

*Tidepool extravaganza*

Black Katy Chiton. Photo: Kim Goldberg

The expanse of tidepools that awaits you here offers one of the best opportunities to view intertidal creatures and plants anywhere on the west coast of North America. The first marine research station in the Pacific Northwest was established here in 1901. For the few short years it existed, the station, operated by the University of Minnesota, drew students and researchers from around the world. As you explore the tidepools carved into the sandstone shelves, notice how different plants and animals occupy different depths, or intertidal zones, depending on how much drying out they can withstand. The small and colonial **Aggregating Anemone** is found higher up than the larger and solitary **Giant Green Anemone**, although both may be visible in the same pool. The **Purple Sea Urchin** is often found above the low-tide line in sandstone pockets it has eroded with its teeth and spines, while **Red** and **Green Sea Urchins** remain at or below the low-tide line. The tidepools also abound with **chitons** (particularly **Black Katy**), colourful **coralline algae** (branching and encrusting), **Shield-backed Kelp Crabs**, **Tidepool Sculpins**, **limpets**, **snails**, **hermit crabs**, **barnacles**, **periwinkles** and much more. Beds of **California Mussels** cover the rocky shelves. Check the Tofino tide tables before you visit. The tide must be no higher than 1.2 metres (4 feet) or you won't have much to look at. For ideal viewing, you want a 0.6-metre (2-foot) tide or lower. In August and September, Botanical Beach is one of the best spots in BC for seeing **Brown Pelicans**.

**DIRECTIONS:** *Drive to Port Renfrew, 107 km northwest of Victoria at the end of Highway 14. When highway ends, turn left on Cerantes Road and proceed 3.2 km to parking lot. Hike the 10-minute trail down to Botanical Beach. Accommodations are limited in Port Renfrew, and reservations are advisable. Overnight parking is permitted in the Botanical Beach parking lot. Do not leave valuables in your car.*

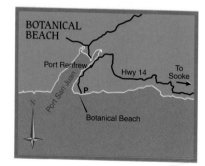

BOTANICAL BEACH

Port Renfrew

Port San Juan

Hwy 14

To Sooke

P

Botanical Beach

Giant Green Anemones gain their colour from
algae that live in their tissues..
Photo: Kim Goldberg

Botanical Beach is the northern terminus of the 47-kilometre Juan de Fuca
Marine Trail, opened in 1996. The trail can also be accessed from Parkinson
Creek, Sombrio Beach and the trail's southern terminus, China Beach Provincial
Park. All of these beaches along the Juan de Fuca Strait can be good for land-
based whale watching, partic-
ularly during **Gray Whale**
migration in April and
December.

Gray Whales and **Killer
Whales** are often spotted off
Botanical Beach throughout
the summer. However, the
best beach for whale watching
is French Beach Provincial
Park, 53 kilometres before
Port Renfrew.

Purple Sea Urchins.
Photo: D.F. Fraser

**BC Parks, South Vancouver Island District:**     250-391-2300

# Swan Lake/ Christmas Hill Nature Sanctuary

*Wildflowers, year-round birdwatching*

*Male Red-winged Blackbird. Photo: David Denning*

Photo: Kim Goldberg

Formed 12,000 years ago when the last glacier receded, Swan Lake today offers excellent birdwatching opportunities year-round. The 2.5-kilometre loop trail with floating boardwalk, wharves and bird blinds gives you easy access to the lake and surrounding upland fields and hedgerows. **Great Blue Heron** can be seen on almost any visit. But keep an eye out for the smaller and much rarer **Green Heron** from June through September. In winter, you can expect **American Wigeon**, **Gadwall**, **Ring-necked Duck**, **Ruddy Duck** and **Pied-billed Grebe**. **Green-winged Teal** and **Northern Shoveler** show up during fall and spring migration. In spring and summer, **Common Yellowthroats** (a warbler with a heavy black mask and yellow throat) and **Red-winged Blackbirds** are abundant around the lake. Look for the small but noisy **Marsh Wrens** perched atop Cattails. **Ring-necked Pheasants** bustle through the surrounding fields that were once farmland.

Swan Lake is one of the best sites in the Victoria region for viewing **Muskrats**. Introduced to Vancouver Island in the 1920s, these mainly herbivorous rodents eat the roots, tubers and stems of Cattails and bulrushes and can remain underwater for up to 20 minutes, gnawing away at plants with their chisel-like incisors. Look for them in Tuesday Pond east of the parking lot or near the floating boardwalk just past the Nature House. **Mink** (the Muskrat's major predator) and **River Otter** may be seen in the lake

**DIRECTIONS:** *From downtown Victoria, drive north on Blanshard, take the McKenzie exit and follow signs to "Nature Sanctuary." From points north of Victoria, follow Highway 1 south, turn left on McKenzie, cross under Highway 17 (Pat Bay Highway) and follow signs to sanctuary.*

year-round, but particularly in winter. From November through April, watch for **Red-tailed Hawk** and **Cooper's Hawk** overhead. On warm days starting in late spring look for **Western Painted Turtles** sunning themselves on partly submerged logs. Sometimes six or more will line up on one log. The Vancouver Island populations of this colourful turtle probably began as pet shop escapees.

The 30-minute hike from Swan Lake to Christmas Hill takes you to a very different terrain of rocky outcroppings and **Garry Oak** forest carpeted with wildflowers in the spring, boasting showy displays of **Common Camas**, **White Fawn Lily**, **Satin-flower** and **Shootingstar**. **Northern Flicker**, **Downy Woodpecker**, **Chestnut-backed Chickadee** and **Brown Creeper** are present in the forested areas throughout the year. Be sure to stop at the nature house and native plant garden near the lake to pick up trail guides and a bird checklist.

*All dragonflies and damselflies have two pairs of long, transparent wings, enabling them to fly, hover and turn with great agility. Dragonflies, like this Cardinal Meadowhawk (Sympetrum illotum), hold their wings outstretched at rest, while damselflies fold their wings parallel to their bodies. Photo: Teresa Shepard*

*Mallard ducklings. Photo: Kim Goldberg*

Swan Lake Christmas Hill Nature Sanctuary:     250-479-0211

# Island View Beach Regional Park

Photo: Kim Goldberg

*Beach life, birds*

Anise Swallowtail. Photo: Trudy Chatwin

Sculpted over the eons by wind and waves, the ever-changing contours of the dunes, berm and sand bars of this 39-hectare park on the Saanich Peninsula present a good example of the coastal beach complex of plants and associated marine life and wildlife. As you walk the berm along the high-water mark you'll find **Beach Pea**, **Kinnikinnick**, the sticky-leaved **Yellow Sand-verbena**, imported **Tree Lupine** (with tall spikes of yellow flowers in summer) and various beach grasses all working to stabilize the shifting sands. In fall and winter, watch for **Short-eared Owl**, **Northern Harrier** and **Red-tailed Hawk** hunting for **Townsend's Voles** in the fields and along the dykes. If you have a spotting scope, scan nearby James Island, where you could see **Fallow Deer** grazing in the fields. This white-spotted deer was imported from Europe at the turn of the century.

On the beach at Island View, look for **Purple Shore Crabs** browsing on decomposing plants and animals under the rocks. Colonies of **Common Acorn Barnacles** cover the larger rocks. In winter, thousands of alcids congregate offshore, primarily **Common Murre**, **Pigeon Guillemot** and **Marbled Murrelet**, along with **Oldsquaw** and other sea ducks. In summer, you may see hundreds of **Rhinoceros Auklet**. All four species of loon have been seen here in winter, although **Common** and **Pacific Loons** are the most frequent. **Surf** and **White-winged Scoters** are also common at this time. To glimpse the lesser seen **Black Scoter**, stroll north on the beach toward Saanichton Spit. **Black Oystercatchers** can be found year-round

**DIRECTIONS:** *From Victoria, take Highway 17 (Pat Bay Highway) approximately 14 km to Island View Road. Turn right and proceed 2.7 km to end, then turn left onto Homathko Drive for the short drive into the parking lot.*

along the shore. Keep an eye out for the sleek heads of **Harbor Seals** bobbing in the water.

Back from the beach and berm you'll find typical field and hedgerow birds in the thickets of **Nootka Rose** and **Pacific Crab Apple**. **Northern Flicker**, **Red-winged Blackbird**, **Song Sparrow** and **White-crowned Sparrow** are likely throughout the year. The trails through the thickets have even produced such rarities as **Mountain Bluebird**, **Lewis's Woodpecker** and **Say's Phoebe**. In winter an occasional **Northern Shrike** turns up in the hawthorn trees and fences in the abandoned farm fields. Unlike typical birds of prey, shrikes (also called "butcher birds") lack strong talons for grasping their prey so they impale their victims on sharp objects and sometimes leave them

*The sticky leaves, stems and flowers of Yellow Sand-verbena trap sand, protecting the plant from drought. Photo: Kim Goldberg*

wedged into tree forks for later consumption. In May and June, look for **Anise Swallowtail** laying eggs on **Lomatium** and other members of the carrot family. As you drive into the park on Island View Road, check Martindale Flats on either side of the road for **Peregrine Falcons** and **Trumpeter Swans** from December to March.

*Cedar Waxwings breed in hedges and thickets here. Photo: Rick Ikona*

| | |
|---|---|
| **Capital Regional District Parks:** | 250-478-3344 |
| **CRD Parks Recorded Information:** | 250-474-PARK |
| **World Wide Web:** | http://vvv.com/crd/<br>parkhome.html |

# Sidney Spit Provincial Marine Park

*Rich saltwater marsh*

Double-crested Cormorants. Photo: BC Environment

Located on Sidney Island 5 kilometres off-shore from the town of Sidney, this long sandspit and adjacent lagoon and campground offer some truly remarkable opportunities for viewing native and exotic species. The lagoon is one of the largest saltwater marshes on the BC coast. Up to one thousand **Brant** may be seen grazing on the subtidal beds of eelgrass during spring migration in March and April en route to their Alaskan breeding grounds. The eelgrass is also a nursing area for young salmon, which are in turn the principal food source for the **Great Blue Heron**. The mudflats are often teeming with shorebirds, including thousands of **Western Sandpiper** during southward migration from July to September and sometimes hundreds of **Black-bellied Plovers** in the fall and winter. There have even been rare sightings of **Marbled Godwit** and **Long-billed Curlew**.

**Common Nighthawks** nest on the ground along the 2-kilometre spit, so be careful where you step from June to August. The well-camouflaged female lays two camouflaged eggs directly on the ground without building a nest. **Bald Eagle**, **Killdeer** and **Belted Kingfisher** are also nesting near the water. As you walk the loop trail through the forest and uplands you may glimpse one of the island's numerous **Fallow Deer**. Their ancestors were imported to nearby James Island from England in the early 1900s and subsequently swam to Sidney Island where they have been having a dramatic impact on vegetation ever since. **Killer Whale**, **Dall's Porpoise**, **Harbor Seal**,

**DIRECTIONS:** *From Victoria, take Highway 17 (Pat Bay Highway) 24 km to Sidney. Foot passenger ferry to Sidney Island is at the end of Beacon Avenue and leaves hourly from mid-May to September. The free public parking lot at the corner of 2nd and Bevan is the best place to leave your car.*

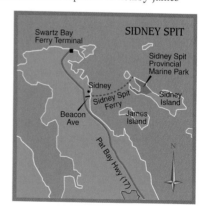

*Pacific Treefrogs breed in the freshwater ponds left over from the old brick works in the park. You will hear their chirping chorus from March to mid-August.*
*Photo: Jay Patterson*

**California Sea Lion**, **Mink** and **River Otter** are commonly seen in the surrounding waters.

The ferry ride over affords good viewing of alcids (a family of seabirds that come ashore only to breed) including **Rhinoceros Auklet**, **Pigeon Guillemot**, **Common Murre** and **Marbled Murrelet**. Alcids are weak flyers and ungainly on land, but they are expert swimmers and divers, using their stubby wings to "fly" underwater in pursuit of herring and other fish. In late summer, watch for spectacular concentrations of alcids and **California** and **Heermann's Gulls** at "ball-ups" of small fish in Sidney Channel. Mandarte Island (a bare, whitish rock visible from the east side of the park) contains one of the largest seabird colonies in Georgia Strait with over 8,000 nesting birds, including **Double-crested** and **Pelagic Cormorants**, **Glaucous-winged Gull**, **Pigeon Guillemot**, **Rhinoceros Auklet** and even a few **Tufted Puffins**.

*Common Nighthawks are more closely related to owls than to hawks. On summer evenings, listen for their nasal "peent" overhead as they swoop and glide with their wide mouths gaping, scooping up hundreds of insects on the wing.*
*Photo: Rick Ikona*

BC Parks, Malahat District:    250-391-2300
Sidney Spit ferry:    250-727-7700

*Photo: Frank Stoney*

# Active Pass

*Wonders of sea,
shore and sky*

Dall's Porpoise. Photo: Frank Stoney

Ferries can serve as excellent observation platforms for wildlife viewing if you choose the right route and season. One of the very best runs for this purpose is the Swartz Bay–Galiano Island ferry because it takes you through the wildlife-rich waters of Active Pass. If you leave your vehicle at the Swartz Bay terminal and board as a foot passenger, you can give yourself a three-hour round-trip wildlife watching cruise for under $5.00. The Swartz Bay–Tsawwassen ferry link to the lower mainland also takes you through Active Pass.

Active Pass is a magnet for waterbirds because vast quantities of small fish and plankton are teeming near the surface. They are pushed up from colder depths by strong tidal currents that are deflected off sedimentary ridges on the ocean floor as water surges through this deep, narrow channel between Galiano and Mayne Islands. A morning cruise during April or May should yield the best viewing opportunities. But any time from October through May could be interesting. Flocks of **Brandt's Cormorants** and **Pacific Loons** sometimes number in the thousands in late winter and early spring. As many as 10,000 **Bonaparte's Gulls** can be present in the pass and just outside the south entrance in April and May. **Common Murre** is also abundant at this time. An occasional **Ancient Murrelet** is possible. Look for **Oldsquaw** and **Red-breasted Merganser** in the waters before you reach the pass. **Common** and **Barrow's Goldeneye** are likely around the Swartz Bay ferry dock. **Bald Eagles** are regularly seen in the pass in winter. More than one hundred were counted from the ferry once in January. Look for them perched in the tall trees along both sides of the channel.

June and July are slow months for birds. Summer birds that you are likely to see include **Glaucous-winged Gull**,

**ACTIVE PASS**

Active Pass

Galiano Island

Mayne Island

Ferry Route

Saltspring Island

Swartz Bay Ferry Terminal

**DIRECTIONS:** *Swartz Bay ferry terminal is located 30 km north of Victoria at the end of Highway 17 (Pat Bay Highway).*

California Gull, **Black Oyster-catcher**, **Pelagic** and **Double-crested Cormorants**, **Pigeon Guillemot**, and possibly **Marbled Murrelet** and **Rhinoceros Auklet**. Check the hills above Active Pass at this time for high flying **Swifts**, **Turkey Vultures** and Bald Eagles. Flocks of **Red-necked Phalarope** have been seen in late August. You should also see **Common Tern** by this time and continuing into September. Look for the terns (which are sometimes being harried by **Parasitic Jaeger** or **Heermann's Gull**) around the north entrance to the pass, near the Sturdies Bay ferry dock on Galiano. **Harbor Seal** is common year-round, and **Killer Whale** and **Dall's Porpoise** are always possible. **Harbor Porpoise** is also in these waters but will usually depart or not surface when boats are present, making it a less common sighting than Dall's Porpoise.

*This two-year-old Bald Eagle will not attain its full adult plumage (brown body, white head and tail, yellow bill) until its fourth or fifth year. Photo: BC Environment*

*Look for Great Blue Heron along the shoreline in Active Pass. Photo: BC Environment*

| BC Ferries (recorded information): | 1-888-223-3779 |
| BC Ferries on World Wide Web: | http://bcferries.bc.ca/ferries |

# Goldstream Provincial Park

*Photo: Kim Goldberg*

*Salmon runs in old-growth forest*

*Northern Pygmy-owl. Photo: BC Environment*

The shallow rapids and easily accessible streambank of Goldstream River give you a front-row seat for viewing an annual salmon run and all the associated wildlife that comes to feed on the eggs and carcasses of spawned-out fish. From mid-October through late December, some 20,000 **salmon** (primarily **Chum** with lesser numbers of **Coho** and **Chinook**) make the journey from the Pacific Ocean up Finlayson Arm of the Saanich Inlet to spawn in the river they were born in 3–4 years earlier. The main activity occurs along a 1-kilometre stretch of river extending from the picnic area to the Freeman King Visitor Centre at the north end of the park. You can watch the female salmon digging her "redd" or trench in the gravelly riverbed and depositing her eggs, while the male stands guard until it's time for him to fertilize the eggs, which the female then covers with gravel. The weak and exhausted salmon die at this point, but for many other species a new food chain has just begun.

Sea-going **Cutthroat Trout** and **Coho** fry are on hand to feast on the eggs not covered by gravel, as are numerous **Mew Gulls** and **American Dippers**. **Dippers** are chunky gray birds that walk underwater to feed. Larger birds and mammals devour thousands of fish carcasses. Up to 2,000 birds (mainly gulls) use the salmon run each year for free meals. **Glaucous-winged**, **Herring** and **Thayer's Gulls** are the most abundant. One or two of the rarer and paler **Glaucous Gull** are usually present. From December through February, dozens of **Bald Eagles** gather in the tall trees adjacent to the estuary beyond the visitor centre. **Common Merganser** and **Common**

GOLDSTREAM

Finlayson Arm
(Saanich Inlet)

Finlayson Arm Rd

Freeman King
Visitor Centre

= Goldstream
Provincial Park

Goldstream River

Hwy 1

Park HQ

Sooke
Lake Rd

**DIRECTIONS:** *Park entrance is 19 km northwest of downtown Victoria on Highway 1.*

The Western Trillium's white flower turns pink or purple with age. Wasps are important dispersers of Trillium seeds. photo: Kim Goldberg

and **Barrow's Goldeneyes** also partake. **Mink** and **River Otter** do most of their scavenging in the early morning. You may even see a **Harbor Seal** or **California Sea Lion** make it beyond the estuary and into the lower reaches of the river. Be sure to walk to the visitor centre, open daily during the salmon run and in the summer, and weekends the rest of the year.

Goldstream Park is a fruitful place for unusual wildlife watching at other times of the year as well. The cool and damp forest floor beneath the old-growth trees along the river contains particularly large populations of gigantic slugs (the native **Banana Slug** plus two European imports), **Western Red-backed Salamanders** and **Rough-skinned Newts**. In early evening from May through September, look for **bats** (**Big Brown**, **Silver-haired** and **Little Brown**) flying slowly over the river pools near the visitor centre where they forage for insects and drink. Despite popular mythology about these much-maligned mammals, none of Vancouver Island's ten bat species dines on blood.

The Western Red-backed Salamander belongs to a family of lungless salamanders (plethodontids) that breathe entirely through the skin and the lining of the mouth. This salamander reaches its highest known population density in Goldstream Provincial Park. Photo: Trudy Chatwin

| | |
|---|---|
| **BC Parks, South Vancouver Island District:** | 250-391-2300 |
| **Freeman King Visitor Centre:** | 250-478-9414 |

Buttertubs Marsh in winter. Photo: Shirley Goldberg

# SECTION 2
# Nanaimo/ Cowichan

# Cowichan Estuary

*Photo: Kim Goldberg*

*Trumpeter swans and other waterbirds*

*Wilson's Phalarope. Photo: BC Environment*

Fed by two rivers (the Cowichan and the Koksilah), this large estuary near Duncan provides critical winter habitat for thousands of waterfowl each year and supports nearly 230 bird species in total. Waterfowl numbers peak in January and February when more than 4,000 birds have been counted in one day. But a visit any time from September through April should offer good birdwatching. The dabbling ducks are the most abundant birds in the estuary, particularly **American Wigeon, Green-winged Teal** and **Northern Pintail**. The most prevalent diving ducks are **Bufflehead, Common Goldeneye** and **Lesser Scaup**. The "dabbler/diver" distinction is important not only to the ducks (because it reduces competition for food), but also for novice birdwatchers who want some shortcuts to identification. Dabblers all belong to the genus *Anas*. They turn "bottoms up" to feed on plants, seeds and snails near the surface. They have large wings relative to their bodies, which enable them to shoot straight out of the water for a vertical take-off when startled. Dabblers are normally found in shallower waters than divers since their food has to be within reach of the surface. Divers have smaller wings, heavier bodies, and legs set farther back for propelling them underwater. Consequently, divers are ungainly on land, and need a running start on water to get airborne.

The Cowichan estuary and surrounding

**DIRECTIONS:** *From Highway 1 in Duncan, head east on Trunk Road (which quickly becomes Tzouhalem Road) for 6.5 km until you see the Ducks Unlimited sign and dyke trail to your left, immediately after a bridge. Take the 30-minute walk out to the estuary. Or continue on Tzouhalem Road for another 1.5 km and turn left onto Westcan's access road to the Cowichan Bay dock. Proceed to the end by car or on foot, passing Koksilah Marsh on your right.*

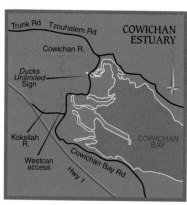

farm fields are some of the most important wintering grounds for **Trumpeter Swans** on Vancouver Island, with maximum daily numbers sometimes exceeding 400. **Killdeer** is the most prevalent shorebird. **Pectoral Sandpiper** can be numerous in the fall. **Bald Eagle** is ever-present, and **Northern Harrier** is commonly seen hunting over the flats and salt marsh. Unlike other raptors, the harrier flies very low over its hunting area, usually just 1–2 metres off the ground. Look for its distinctive white rump patch. Harriers are particularly active over the salt marsh to your left along the far end of the Ducks Unlimited dyke trail. There has been at least one winter

*The tiny Marsh Wren is prominent in spring and summer when it perches atop Cattails to sing. Photo: Katherine Ikona*

sighting of the very unusual **Black-crowned Night Heron** in the slough you pass on your left before the salt marsh. **Great Blue Heron** is common throughout the estuary. In spring and summer be alert for the rarer and more secretive **Green Heron** lurking in brushy margins along waterways. At this time you can also see the **Purple Martins** nesting in boxes on the estuary and along the right (south) side of the Westcan access road. The rare **Wilson's Phalarope** has also nested in this part of the estuary.

*Osprey, like this adult and juvenile, nest at Cowichan Estuary.*
*Photo: BC Environment*

# Cowichan River Dyke Trail

*River mammals, herons, rare birds*

*Violet-green Swallow. Photo: Steve Baillie*

Photo: Kim Goldberg

This fine example of a **Black Cottonwood** riparian zone along the banks of the Cowichan River in Duncan supports a diverse number of birds and other animals, including at least three rare "regulars," due to the varied habitat. In addition to the fast-flowing river with its cobblestone bottom, the dyke trail also takes you past a slow and shady creek, an eerily mysterious Everglades-like pond, and the city's sewage lagoons, which are a magnet for wintering waterfowl. The pond behind the Freshwater Eco-Centre parking lot is one of the better places on Vancouver Island to see the rare **Green Heron**. Three or four reside here (nesting nearby), accounting for approximately one-third of the known population in the Cowichan Valley—the unofficial Green Heron capital of Vancouver Island. Both the Green Heron and the larger **Great Blue Heron** are on the provincial government's Blue List of species considered vulnerable and at risk in BC. The pond is also a good place to see **Wood Ducks**, which are nesting in boxes and cavities in the cottonwood trees.

The second unusual species that birdwatchers come here in search of is **Franklin's Gull** at the sewage lagoons. Each fall, one lone bird (but always in its first winter plumage, which means it's a different bird each year) turns up among the similar-looking **Bonaparte's Gulls**. Most Franklin's Gulls migrate from their breeding grounds on the Canadian prairies due south to their wintering grounds in Central and South America, never coming near our coast. The other unusual bird seen with some regularity on the sewage lagoons in winter is **Tufted Duck**, an Old World species look-

**DIRECTIONS:** *From Highway 1 in Duncan, turn east onto Trunk Road (first stoplight north of steel bridge). Proceed straight onto Marchmont Road, following blue signs to Freshwater Eco-Centre. Dyke trail begins at parking lot. From the trail, sewage lagoons are to the left, Cowichan River to the right.*

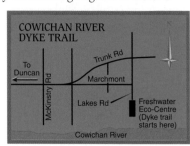

COWICHAN RIVER
DYKE TRAIL

To Duncan

Trunk Rd

McKinstry Rd

Marchmont

Lakes Rd

Freshwater Eco-Centre (Dyke trail starts here)

Cowichan River

ing similar to our scaup and Ring-necked Duck.

While walking the riverside trail and the signed interpretive trail along the dyke, be alert for the river-associated mammals that live here, including **Mink**, **Raccoon**, **River Otter** and **Muskrat**. **Rough-skinned Newt** and **Pacific Treefrog** are also present. **Violet-green** and **Tree Swallows** nest in the small boxes and cavities you see on the cotton-woods. In the summer you can watch showy **Western Tiger Swallowtails** pollinating **Large-leaved Lupine** in the meadow between the dyke and riverside trail.

*At rest, the Tree Swallow is readily distin-guished from the Violet-green Swallow (opposite) by the dark helmet completely covering the eye. The Violet-green Swallow's helmet arches above its eye.*
*Photo: Steve Baillie*

**Pale Tiger Swallowtail** is also present. The heron pond and small stream are known to locals as "Fish Gut Alley" because they are littered with salmon car-casses during the fall spawning of **Coho** and **Chum**. The spawning, which you can watch beside the Eco-Centre, attracts **Bald Eagles**, gulls and other wildlife. The event reaches its peak in the second week of November but continues to the end of December. Be sure to visit the Freshwater Eco-Centre for a local checklist and to view the excellent displays on our freshwater environment.

*More than one hundred Wood Ducks (male shown) can be found on the sewage lagoons in late summer and early fall.*
*Photo: Frank Stoney*

**Freshwater Eco-Centre:** 250-746-6722

# Somenos Marsh

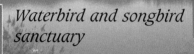

Photo: Kim Goldberg

*Waterbird and songbird sanctuary*

*Canada Goose. Photo: Steve Baillie*

Nearly 200 bird species rely on this rich wetland ecosystem whose pond, lake, creek and seasonally flooded fields provide crucial winter habitat for **Mallard**, **Canada Goose**, **American Wigeon**, **Trumpeter Swan**, **Gadwall**, **Northern Shoveler**, **Northern Pintail**, **Green-winged Teal** and many other waterfowl. **Great Blue Heron** and **Belted Kingfisher** are common year-round. **Wood Duck** and **Hooded Merganser** nest in tree cavities. In 1996, the rare **Green Heron** also nested here behind the BC Forest Museum at the north end of the refuge. Four young herons hatched, and the family was regularly seen throughout the summer in the Ducks Unlimited pond below the museum, visible from the highway. **Beaver** are active at the back side of the pond, and **River Otter** are common throughout the area. As you scan the flocks of **American Wigeon** present from October through April, keep an eye out for a rare **Eurasian Wigeon** (male has creamy cap and reddish-brown head and neck).

In winter, always check the bird feeders along the boardwalk out to the blind. **Spotted Towhee**, **Dark-eyed Junco** and various **sparrows** (especially **Song**, **Fox** and **Golden-crowned**) are frequent diners there. As you approach the blind in summer, you may flush a **Common Snipe**, which takes to the air with a harsh "*skipe*" cry and a zigzagging flight pat-

**DIRECTIONS:** *The refuge is located 1 km north of Duncan on Highway 1. A future parking lot is planned for the southeast edge of the refuge, across Beverly Street from the Canadian Tire store. Until then, drive 500 metres north of Beverly Street on Highway 1 and turn right onto the short, unmarked laneway. Park and walk across the empty lot to the trail to the viewing blind. Or drive 1 km farther north on Highway 1 to the roadside pull-out.*

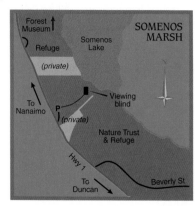

*The Green Heron has only been a breeding resident on Vancouver Island since the 1960s. Photo: D.F. Fraser*

tern. In early June, look overhead for migrating **Black** and **Vaux's Swifts**, which sometimes number in the hundreds. Swifts look like swallows with very long wings, although they are actually more closely related to hummingbirds.

Somenos Creek, which flows from the south end of Somenos Lake, is exceptionally good for **Black-headed Grosbeak** from June to September. You may see them from the blind if you scan the willows bordering the creek. In winter, **Peregrine Falcons** are occasionally seen hunting from the woodlands by the creek. In February 1996, a Peregrine was observed chasing a much rarer **Gyrfalcon** across the creek, creating considerable excitement among local birdwatchers as this was the first record of Gyrfalcon at Somenos. Since the mid-1990s, Somenos has become a major spring migration stopover for **Greater White-fronted Geese** and **Canada Geese**. Under the right weather conditions, up to 2,000 Greater White-fronted Geese will touch down here to feed and rest between mid-April and early May before flying to Tofino on Vancouver Island's west coast and then north to their Alaskan breeding grounds. Even greater numbers of Canada Geese have been seen.

*Look for Canvasbacks from October to March. Photo: BC Environment*

**Somenos Marsh Wildlife Society: 250-746-8383**

# Green Mountain

*Photo: Katherine Ikona*

*Wildflower-carpeted slopes, marmots*

*Gray Jay. Photo: Steve Baillie*

Situated 30 kilometres southwest of Nanaimo, Green Mountain offers excellent opportunities to observe and photograph sub-alpine wildflowers and animals. From spring through fall, look for **Golden Eagle**, **Bald Eagle**, **Band-tailed Pigeon**, **Gray Jay**, **Steller's Jay** and **Varied Thrush**. In August and September, as many as 50 **Roosevelt Elk** can sometimes be found grazing on the mountain's steep, sloping meadows. You may even witness a bull elk bugling to attract other elk and to assert his dominance over the herd. This is also good terrain for **Black Bear** and **Cougar**.

But the most intriguing residents on Green Mountain are the endangered **Vancouver Island Marmots**. Fewer than 200 of these gregarious creatures remain on the planet, and they are restricted to just a few mountains on central Vancouver Island. They live colonially in extended family groups on steep, sub-alpine slopes where they hibernate in burrows beneath a deep, insulating blanket of snow from September or early October until April or mid-May. The marmots on Green Mountain have been studied extensively since the 1980s and can be viewed from May to September at the steep, rocky slope at the summit. You

••••••••••••••••••••••••••••••••••••••••••••••••••••••••••••••••••••••••••••

*Directions: The site is accessed via Timber West logging roads, which can only be used by the public on weekends. Drive 10 km south of Nanaimo on Highway 1, and take the Nanaimo Lakes turn-off. Proceed about 20 minutes until you come to the Timber West gate, where you must sign in and pay a $5 fee on your first visit. Continue on the main, paved logging road. At the first major fork (by the old green building), bear left. After about 3 km, take the first road to the left (marked "K15") and follow it about 3 km uphill. When you come to a hairpin turn to the left (marked by a "K30" sign pointing left), turn right and continue up that road toward the summit. The road is passable by 4-wheel-drive and will get you within a 45-minute hike to the summit. Low-slung vehicles should park back at the "K30" intersection, from which it's a 2- to 3-hour hike to the summit.*

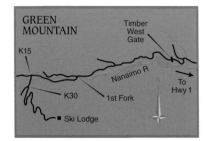

GREEN MOUNTAIN

Timber West Gate

K15

K30

1st Fork

Nanaimo R

Ski Lodge

To Hwy 1

Vancouver Island Marmot.
Photo: Katherine Ikona

may also notice marmots along the road on your way up, where they have taken to burrowing into the side-castings of road construction.

Do not visit the Green Mountain meadows with large groups of people, unleashed dogs or all-terrain vehicles, which can destroy the lush carpet of grasses and wildflowers the marmots feast on. This is a Critical Wildlife Management Area, so tread lightly!

The Vancouver Island Marmot is one of the rarest animals on earth and has been designated an endangered species both provincially and federally. Clearcut logging may be contributing to the species' decline by luring dispersing sub-adults into food-rich habitat in the spring and summer, where they don't overwinter as successfully, and where predators such as Cougar and **Gray Wolf** find it easier to hunt marmots. A government-sponsored recovery project is underway with the goal of someday removing the Vancouver Island Marmot from the endangered species list. The first marmot transplant occurred in 1996, when six marmots were moved from a clearcut to a former sub-alpine marmot colony near Port Alberni. European marmots, which were eliminated from parts of Austria, Germany, France and Switzerland earlier this century, have now rebuilt their populations as a result of postwar transplanting.

There are fewer Vancouver Island Marmots in the world than Giant Pandas. Photo: Trudy Chatwin

| | |
|---|---|
| **Ministry of Environment, Lands and Parks:** | 250-751-3100 |
| **Timber West** *(to confirm gate access):* | 250-246-6811 |
| **Vancouver Island Marmot Home Page:** | http://www.islandnet.com/~marmot/homepage.html |

# Nanaimo River Estuary

*Waterfowl riches, purple martins*

Osprey. Photo: Rick Ikona

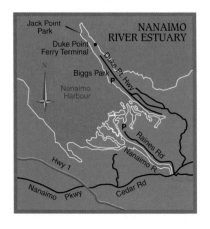

Located at the south end of the Nanaimo Harbour, the Nanaimo River estuary (BC's fifth largest estuary) is an important wintering ground and migratory stopover for waterfowl. Look for the elegant **Trumpeter Swans** from November to March along with **Horned** and **Pied-billed Grebes**, **Bufflehead**, **Barrow's** and **Common Goldeneye**, **Northern Pintail**, **Green-winged Teal**, **Surf Scoter**, **Greater Scaup** and **American Wigeon**. Throughout the year you can expect **Great Blue Heron**, **Canada Goose**, **Mallard**, **Osprey**, **Bald Eagle**, **Red-tailed Hawk**, **Harbor Seal** and **River Otter**. **Turkey Vultures** gliding overhead are common in the summer and into September. If you're lucky, you may even spot a **Peregrine Falcon** or the smaller **Merlin** hawking over the estuary. **Purple Martins** (large, dark swallows) are nesting in martin boxes on the pilings along the city side (Haliburton Street) of the estuary. The Nanaimo martin colony has been so successful that a spin-off population has been nesting in martin boxes on nearby Newcastle Island since 1995. Purple Martins are currently on the provincial government's Red List of threatened or endangered species.

The Nanaimo estuary's claim to wildlife fame extends back through the eons. In 1996, while building a road for the Duke Point ferry terminal, construction workers unearthed a 72-million-year-old fossil of a flowering tropical palm (Canada's largest intact fossil of a leaf of *Phoenicites imperialis*, measuring nearly two metres across) and an equally important fossil of an intermediate plant

**DIRECTIONS** *to Biggs Park: 6 km south of Nanaimo on Highway 1 take the Cedar turn-off at the stoplight and proceed to Duke Point ferry terminal. Biggs Park is on road to terminal, about 1 km before end.*

between ferns and flowering plants (*Nilssonia sp.*).

There is unofficial access to the estuary from the end of Raines Road (left off Cedar Road immediately after crossing the bridge over the Nanaimo River). However, the best public vantage point is the Biggs Park trail leading to Jack Point Park next to the Duke Point ferry terminal. The 800-metre shoreline trail from Biggs Park offers an unobstructed view across the estuary (mudflats at low tide). The loop trail through Jack Point Park at the end takes you through a **Garry Oak**,

*Erecting Purple Martin boxes in estuaries and harbours has proven to be an extremely effective method for expanding the breeding range of this particular bird on southeastern Vancouver Island, as evidenced by the colonies in Nanaimo harbour, Ladysmith harbour, Cowichan estuary and other locations. Photo: D.F. Fraser*

**Arbutus** and **Douglas-fir** forest, opening onto a rocky point and curving back along the Northumberland Channel (page 58), which can be busy with **Northern** and **California Sea Lions** from November to March. Along the forest trail expect **Chestnut-backed Chickadee**, **Golden-crowned Kinglet**, **Dark-eyed Junco**, **Bushtit** and **Song Sparrow**.

*Trumpeter Swans remain gray-brown for their first year. Photo: Katherine Ikona*

# Northumberland Channel

*Best place to watch sea lions*

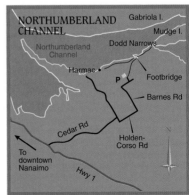

Northern (Steller's) Sea Lion. Photo: Steve Baillie

Photo: Steve Baillie

Each year from November to March, thousands of **California** and **Northern Sea Lions** converge in Georgia Strait anticipating the December arrival and March spawning of vast schools of Pacific Herring. With gulls screaming and wheeling overhead, **Bald Eagles** lining up by the dozens in treetops, and the endless honking of sea lions, this noisy, malodorous feeding frenzy is one of the island's premier wildlife spectacles. Getting a good view of the sea lions from land can be tricky, but one notable exception is the log booms near the Harmac pulp mill just south of Nanaimo in the Northumberland Channel. Historically, hundreds of male sea lions (predominantly California) parked their hefty haunches here each winter.

Because sea lions follow the prey population, the exact location of the majority of them in the strait changes every 5–6 years as the herring shift their movement. Sea lion numbers at the Harmac log booms peaked in the late 1980s and early 1990s when 2,000 would congregate here annually. Prior to that, their largest concentration had been farther south in the strait at Porlier Pass. Since the

**DIRECTIONS** *to hiking trail: 6 km south of Nanaimo on Highway 1, take the Cedar turn-off at the stoplight and proceed toward the Duke Point ferry terminal. After 4.2 km, take the signed turn-off to the right for Cedar, then turn left onto Holden-Corso Road by the Millway store at the sign for Cable Bay Trail. Proceed along Holden-Corso (which becomes Barnes Road) for 3.3 km. Take Nicola Road to the left and proceed straight to parking lot at the end. Follow the signed 2-km trail to the Cable Bay footbridge. To view the log booms, take the path to the left **without** crossing the footbridge and walk for 10–15 minutes. To view Dodd Narrows, cross the bridge, take the right-hand trail at the fork and follow it for 15–20 minutes.*

mid-1990s, they have moved up the strait, making the south end of Denman and Hornby islands their smorgasbord of choice, although more than 100 turned up on the Harmac booms in winter 1996–97.

Back in 1990, about 100 of the boldest beasts left the booms and began invading Harmac's boom boats and work platforms, knocking over equipment and coating everything with a thick, slippery, smelly layer of excrement. The company tried to deter the squatters with noisemakers, strobe lights, a low-voltage electric fence and even a water cannon. The sea lions ignored the noisemakers and lights, knocked the fence down and lay on it, and thought the cannon made a great new water sport. Recognizing a superior adversary, Harmac capitulated to the incredible hulks. The company began hosting an annual sea lion festival for one weekend in January with on-site displays and boat rides. The festival was cancelled in 1997 for financial reasons, but may resume in the future. The rest of the

*California Sea Lions journey up the coast from breeding colonies off California. Photo: Steve Baillie*

time, you can get a fairly good look from shore by following the trail directions below. Bring your binoculars or spotting scope. The long island you see directly across from the booms is Gabriola. Bald Eagles, **Peregrine Falcons**, **Pelagic Cormorants** and **Pigeon Guillemots** nest on its steep cliffs. Dodd Narrows is a narrow tidal surge channel with extremely strong currents running between Vancouver Island and Mudge Island, which sometimes affords close-up viewing of sea lions feeding in winter.

California Sea Lions are easily distinguished from the much larger Northern (also called Steller's) Sea Lion by their size: a mere 270 kilograms maximum as opposed to the 900-kilogram bulk of a male Northern. California (the circus "seal") is also darker—black when wet—and has a steep, almost vertical forehead compared to the Northern's low, flattish forehead.

| Nanaimo Travel Infocentre: | 250-756-0106 (for festival dates and information) |
|---|---|

# Nanaimo Waterfront Promenade

*Teeming tidepools and birds galore*

Red-breasted Merganser. Photo: D.F. Fraser

Nanaimo's 4-kilometre seaside walkway, extending from the busy boat basin downtown to the BC Ferries terminal in Departure Bay, often affords excellent, up-close viewing of numerous birds and marine life. Beginning at the boat basin, look for schools of **Threespine Stickleback**, glinting silver in the sun, and the larger **Shiner Perch** and **Pile Perch** around the docks in summer. Small **Moon Jellyfish** are fairly common in the summer and, if you're lucky, you may even see a small school of **Opalescent Squid** (the type you usually encounter frozen in the market) swimming near the surface beside the wharves. At low tide, the **Ochre Sea Star** (which can range in colour from yellow or orange to purple, brown and red) is exposed on large rocks in the boat basin. Beneath the surface at low tide you can see **Leather Star** and **Shield-backed Kelp Crab** on the rocks and dozens of enormous **Frilled Anemones** attached to the pilings beneath the loading dock.

Just beyond the retail shops, **Canada Geese** and **Belted Kingfisher** are regulars around the Lighthouse Pub and Bistro. The kingfisher is not a shy bird, but you will often hear its loud, rattling call before you see it. Proceed to Swy-a-lana Lagoon with its series of concrete tidepools and stairs descending down to the low-tide zone. The pools abound with **Yellow Shore Crab** (also called Green Shore Crab), **Tidepool Sculpin** (incorrectly called "bullheads"), **chitons**, **limpets**, colourful **encrusting sponges**, **Giant Pacific Oysters** (introduced from Japan in the early 1900s) and much more.

· · · · · · · · · · · · · · · · · · · · · · · · · · · · ·

**DIRECTIONS:** *Nanaimo's boat basin is across the road from the back side of Harbour Park Mall (fronting on highway) in downtown Nanaimo.*

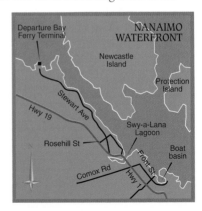

Shortly past the wharf for the ferry to Newcastle, you will come to the mouth of the Millstone River with a footbridge spanning it. The channel separating the two banks of the Millstone estuary is a good place to see **Harbor Seal** and **River Otter** when the tide is reasonably high. At lower tide, you are practically guaranteed to see **Great Blue Heron** fishing in the channel. Across the footbridge, the waters become very productive for **American Wigeon, Surf Scoter** and **Red-breasted Merganser** from fall through spring. The male Red-breasted "merg" is one of our most dazzling species with his shaggy green head, red-orange bill, white collar, speckled reddish-brown chest and striking black-and-white wing markings. Look for **Black Oystercatchers** fossicking among

*Look for Belted Kingfisher perched atop ship masts, lamp standards and pilings. Only the female has the red belly band. Photo: D.F. Fraser*

the rocks at low tide. In the hedges and thickets lining the trail, **Song Sparrow** is a year-round resident, **White-crowned Sparrow** is common in spring and summer, and **Golden-crowned Sparrow** can occasionally be found from fall through spring.

*Ochre Sea Star, also called Purple Star, can be prolific in the boat basin and the rocky outer edge of Swy-a-lana Lagoon at low tide. Photo: Katherine Ikona*

# Newcastle Island Provincial Marine Park

*Photo: Shirley Goldberg*

*Idyllic 306-hectare island park*

*Female Hooded Merganser. Photo: D.F. Fraser*

Located in Nanaimo Harbour, this exceptional 306-hectare park boasts a wide variety of woodland and shoreline birds and other animals, as well as some fascinating remnants of human history. As you disembark from the ferry, look for the island's resident **Canada Geese** to your right grazing on the grassy slopes running down to the water. **Black Oystercatchers** are commonly seen along the shoreline poking their chisel-like red bills among rocks in search of mollusks. Further along the shoreline, which hugs the narrow gap (exposed at low tide) separating Newcastle from Protection Island, look for **Great Blue Heron** year-round and for **Surf Scoter, Barrow's** and **Common Goldeneyes** and other sea ducks in winter. As you leave the campground to your left, the tidal stream you cross is a favourite feeding ground for **Raccoon** and **River Otter**. Early morning and evenings are their most active times. You may even see one of Newcastle's **blonde Raccoons**, a genetic variation that lacks the gene to produce dark colouration. **Bald Eagle** and **Belted Kingfisher** can be expected anywhere along the 9-kilometre perimeter trail. Just past Kanaka Bay, look for **Harbor Seals** bobbing in the water around McKay Point.

The trail to Mallard Lake takes you through a mixed Douglas-fir forest filled with **Chestnut-backed Chickadee, Golden-crowned** and **Ruby-crowned Kinglets, Brown Creeper, Winter Wren** and Canada's largest woodpecker, the **Pileated Woodpecker**. Look closely at the large mounds of fir needles and dirt

**DIRECTIONS:** *Foot-passenger ferry (10-minute ride) departs hourly, May to October, from wharf in Maffeo Sutton Park behind Civic Arena just north of downtown Nanaimo. Moorage is available at Newcastle for boaters and paddlers.*

NEWCASTLE ISLAND

Departure Bay Ferry Terminal

Newcastle Island Provincial Park

Protection island

Hwy 19

Stewart Ave

Ferry

Comox Rd

Front St

Civic Arena

piled off the trail. You will notice the entire surface is moving, for these are huge colonies of **Red Ants**. The lake itself was artificially created and **Beaver** were introduced in the 1930s by one of the island's previous owners, Canadian Pacific Railway. Sharing the lake with the Beaver are **Muskrat, Rough-skinned Newts** and colourful, but hard to spot, **Pumpkin Seed Sunfish**. In February, up to two dozen **Hooded Mergansers** court on the lake.

On the other side of Newcastle, the Channel Trail (facing Nanaimo) takes you by most of the historical sites. For centuries, Salish Indians occupied two villages on the island each year from September through April. Their shell middens are still visible at Midden Bay. The island got its current name from the British miners brought in to mine coal from the 1850s until 1887. Sizable remnants also exist of the island's sandstone quarry, which supplied blocks and pillars for the US Mint in San Francisco, and pulpstone quarry. A Japanese herring saltery and shipyard were operational north of Shaft Point from 1910 until 1941.

*The Rufous Hummingbird (male shown) is attracted to anything red.*
*Its arrival in late March and early April on Vancouver Island and Newcastle*
*Island coincides with the blooming of Red-flowering Currant (inset) and*
*Salmonberry.*
*Photo: Frank Stoney*
*Inset photo: Kim Goldberg*

| BC Parks, South Vancouver Island District: | 250-391-2300 |
| Newcastle Island Ferry: | 250-753-5141 |

# Buttertubs Marsh

*Paradise for birdwatchers*

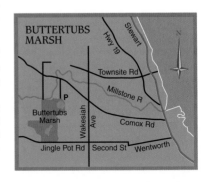

Spotted Towhee. Photo: Steve Baillie

Photo: Kim Goldberg

Just 2 kilometres from downtown Nanaimo you'll find a birdwatcher's oasis and outdoor classroom. This particular site is ideal for expert birders as well as beginners. The experts come in search of the marsh's "specialities," including **American Bittern** and **Virginia Rail**, while "birders in training" will have a good opportunity to see and identify numerous species at close range in any season. Buttertubs is a noisy place in spring and summer when the buzzy song of the **Marsh Wren**, the squeaky whistles from large flocks of **Red-winged Blackbirds**, and the twittering call of **Tree** and **Violet-green Swallows** join the usual chorus of **Mallards** and **Canada Geese**. If you wait patiently at dusk you're likely to see **Beaver** and **Muskrat** coursing through the water. That loud smack you hear is a Beaver slapping its broad tail on the surface before diving.

Buttertubs is one of the best places on Vancouver Island to see and hear the resident but elusive American Bittern. Its odd "*k-dunk*" call is likened to the hollow groan of a rusty pump. This brown-and-white-streaked bird is a master of camouflage, blending so perfectly with marsh vegetation that you may train your binoculars directly on one and still not see it. When alarmed, the bittern will often freeze with its head and bill pointing straight up, increasing the "disappearing" effect. At any time of the year you are certain to see the bittern's larger cousin, the **Great Blue Heron**. As you walk the perimeter trail, watch for **Downy** and **Hairy Woodpeckers** and **Northern Flicker** foraging on the large, flooded oaks along the west dyke.

In winter, the two viewing platforms offer

- - - - - - - - - - - - - - - - - - - - - - - - - -

**DIRECTIONS:** *Just north of downtown Nanaimo, at the intersection of Highway 1 and Comox Road by the Tally Ho Hotel, turn onto Comox Road (which becomes Bowen Road). Drive 2.2 km and turn left on Buttertubs Drive. Parking lot is at end.*

**BUTTERTUBS MARSH**

Hwy 19 · Stewart
Townsite Rd
Millstone R
Buttertubs Marsh · Wakesiah Ave · Comox Rd
Jingle Pot Rd · Second St · Wentworth
P

a good vantage point to observe **Ring-necked Duck, Gadwall, Hooded Merganser, American Wigeon, American Coot** and the occasional **Northern Shoveler**. Also in winter, keep a lookout for a showy **Bohemian Waxwing** among the **Cedar Waxwings** plucking scarlet berries off the Common Hawthorns along the southeast side. In May and June, the marsh is aglow with a spectacular display of **Yellow-flag iris**. Hidden among the reeds is one of the largest populations of Virginia Rails on Vancouver Island. But you're more likely to hear the metallic "*kid-ick, kid-ick*" call of this secretive bird than to see one. Rails eat stalk-climbing snails, other aquatic invertebrates and seeds. Serious birders go out with their "rail tape" and cassette player to call the bird out. Buttertubs is an active nesting area for Mallards, Canada Geese, **Pied-billed Grebes** and other waterfowl in the spring and summer, so keep to the trails and keep dogs leashed.

*The lobed toes of the American Coot, which spends its time swimming and walking on mud, are a compromise between the webbed feet of aquatic birds and the thin claws of land-lubbers. Photo: Kim Goldberg*

*Cattails provide important habitat or food for Marsh Wrens, Red-winged Blackbirds, Muskrats and waterfowl.*
*Photo: Kim Goldberg*

# Morrell Nature Sanctuary

*Photo: Kim Goldberg*

*Grouse, woodpeckers, owls and more*

*Steller's Jay. Photo: Frank Stoney*

A network of well-marked, easy trails winds through this 111-hectare forested sanctuary of mature Douglas-fir, Western Redcedar and Bigleaf Maple with a pond and small lake. The numbered posts on the Rocky Knoll/Beaver Pond trail and the Yew Loop trail are keyed to interpretive brochures you can pick up onsite in summer at the Woods Room Interpretive Centre. In the off-season, brochures are available from sanctuary headquarters 300 metres farther along Nanaimo Lakes Road.

The stillness of winter gives way to song and bustle in the spring and early summer when **Hutton's Vireo, Western Tanager** and numerous warblers—including **Townsend's, Wilson's, Yellow, Yellow-rumped** and **MacGillivray's**—are present. As you stroll the forest trails, listen for the rhythmic hammering of the **Pileated Woodpecker**. Those deep, rectangular holes you see on Western Redcedar trees are the work of this large woodpecker. You may also hear the drumming of a male **Ruffed Grouse** in spring as he stands erect on his drumming log and beats his wings rapidly to attract females. Female grouse with chicks have been encountered on the trails in summer. You'll probably hear the **Red Squirrel's** ratchet-like call before you see it. Or you may just find the squirrel's dinner leftovers—a "cone cob" consisting of a Douglas-fir cone chewed down to the core, lying amid a pile of bracts. Look for the tiny **Red-breasted Nuthatch** walking down tree trunks head-first, or listen for its nasal "*yank, yank, yank.*" **Northwestern Crow, Common**

**DIRECTIONS:** *From the Civic Arena on the highway in downtown Nanaimo, turn onto Comox Road (which becomes Bowen Road) by the Tally Ho Hotel. Follow it to Wakesiah Avenue and turn left. Proceed past Fifth Street and take the next right on Nanaimo Lakes Road. Sanctuary entrance is on right in 1.2 km.*

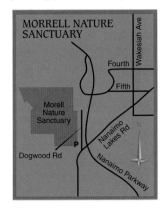

MORRELL NATURE SANCTUARY

Wakesiah Ave

Fourth

Fifth

Morrell Nature Sanctuary

Nanaimo Lakes Rd

Dogwood Rd

Nanaimo Parkway

Raven, Great Horned Owl, Barred Owl, Red-breasted Sapsucker and Spotted Towhee are also present.

Throughout the year, the beaver pond is one of the best places in the region to see **Wood Ducks**. Ducklings are often spotted in the pond in May. **Mallard, Hooded Merganser** and **Belted Kingfisher** are likely year-round. Look for **Bufflehead** from November through April. If you see a large flash of blue in the forest margins near the shore, it's the **Steller's Jay. Great Blue Heron** and **Bald Eagle** are possible anytime.

*The Spotted Tree Borer (Synaphaeta guexi), found here, is a long-horned wood-boring beetle whose larvae tunnel into pines and other trees. Photo: Jay Patterson*

**Beaver** are often active in the pond and farther down the trail at Morrell Lake. The sanctuary has no resident Black Bears or Cougars, but there are rare sightings of each throughout the year, so follow the bear and cougar precautions on page 20.

*Long-toed Salamanders are usually seen here only in breeding season (late winter) and spend the rest of the time underground, hiding in crevices or rotten logs. Photo: Katherine Ikona*

**Morrell Sanctuary Society and Office:** 250-753-5811

# Piper's Lagoon

*Rocky, forested haven
for birds*

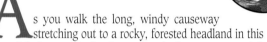

Barrow's Goldeneye. Photo: Frank Stoney

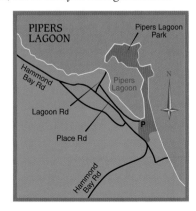

A s you walk the long, windy causeway stretching out to a rocky, forested headland in this Nanaimo city park, you might be surprised to learn that the lagoon to your left was once a whaling station. Over a three-month period between 1907 and 1908, 97 Humpback Whales were killed in Georgia Strait and brought here for processing. As a result, these magnificent baleen (filter feeding) whales have long since disappeared from Georgia Strait, although they are still occasionally seen along the west coast of Vancouver Island and the upper northeast coast (Queen Charlotte Strait).

Today the park is a favourite spot for local birdwatchers and flower lovers. In winter, expect to see **Horned**, **Red-necked** and **Western Grebes** on the ocean side along with **Bufflehead**, **Common Merganser**, **Pigeon Guillemot**, **Common** and **Pacific Loons** and **Surf Scoter**. **California** and **Northern (Steller's) Sea Lions** are present in winter, and **Harbor Seal** is likely any time. Look for **Black Oystercatcher** along the shoreline and **Harlequin Duck** on the water between the headland and Shack Islands. The shacks were occupied by rowboat fishermen in the early 1920s, then by miners during the Depression. You can walk across to the shacks at low tide, but be sure you don't get stranded!

The lagoon can be good for **Red-breasted Merganser**, **Barrow's Goldeneye**, **Black-bellied Plover**, **Killdeer**, **Long-billed** and **Short-billed Dowitchers** and

....................................

**DIRECTIONS:** *From downtown Nanaimo, drive north on highway (Terminal Avenue) and turn right onto Departure Bay Road. After 2 km turn right onto Hammond Bay Road. Proceed 3 km on Hammond Bay, turn right onto Lagoon Road at sign for Piper's Lagoon, then make another right onto Place Road.
Parking lot is at end*

PIPERS LAGOON

Pipers Lagoon Park

Hammond Bay Rd

Pipers Lagoon

Lagoon Rd

N

Place Rd

P

Hammond Bay Rd

Greater and **Lesser Yellowlegs**. **Belted Kingfisher**, **Great Blue Heron** and **Bald Eagle** are present year-round. The causeway is one of the best places in the region to see **Savannah Sparrow** from April to October. Look for yellow between the eye and bill.

At the end of the causeway you'll find a grove of wind-gnarled **Garry Oaks**, some 200 years old, on the rocky knoll to your right and more on the rocky headland to your left. Garry Oak meadows and woodlands are one of the rarest and most endangered habitats in Canada due to urban development and introduced plants such as Scotch Broom. Because these graceful trees require a near-Mediterranean climate, their entire Canadian distribution is limited to the rainshadow territory of southeastern Vancouver Island, the adjacent Gulf Islands and three isolated groves on BC's lower mainland. In April and May the forest is

*Sea Blush and White Fawn Lilies (also inset).*
*Photo: Trudy Chatwin*
*Inset photo: Kim Goldberg*

carpeted with **White Fawn Lily**, **Chocolate Lily**, **Common Camas**, **Menzies' Larkspur** and **Sea Blush**. Look for **Pileated Woodpecker**, **Bewick's Wren** and **Golden-crowned Kinglet** in the Douglas-fir forest on the headland.

*Long-billed Dowitchers.*
*Photo: BC Environment*

# Nanoose Hill

*Flowers, raptors, waterfowl*

Photo: Kim Goldberg

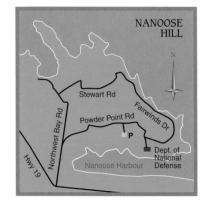

Fairyslipper orchid. Photo: Kim Goldberg

N anoose Hill offers one of Vancouver Island's finest examples of a mixed **Garry Oak–Arbutus** forest. The dry southern-exposure meadows and bluffs of Nanoose Hill overlooking Nanoose Bay are famous among local hikers and naturalists for their profusion of spring wildflowers. In April and May, the sloping meadows are awash in **Common** and **Great Camas**, **Meadow Death-camas**, **Spring-gold** and **Western Buttercup**. **Naked Broomrape** also occurs here, a flowering plant that lives by parasitizing the roots of other plants. In June, watch for the tissuey yellow blooms of the **Brittle Prickly-pear Cactus** (proving just how dry this rainshadow area is). The dark, wooded trails leading up the hill contain the delicate **Fairyslipper orchid**.

Nanoose Hill is one of your better bets on Vancouver Island for spotting **Northern Alligator Lizard**, particularly in May and June. For the lizard's sake you should avoid capturing it, as its tail may break off. It's best to let the lizard reserve that trick for a real predator attack. The hill is also good for watching **Turkey Vultures** and other raptors as they ride the thermal updrafts on their spring and fall migrations. Turkey Vultures (BC's only vulture) are readily distinguished from Bald Eagles in flight by their small heads, their constant tippy

**DIRECTIONS:** *For the hill, drive 24 km north of Nanaimo on Highway 19 to Nanoose and turn right onto Northwest Bay Road at the stoplight. Proceed 1.2 km, turn right onto Powder Point Road, and proceed another 3.5 km to the Notch Park parking lot on your right. (If you come to a turn-off into a military installation, you just missed it.) Proceed by foot up the dirt road until it dead-ends with a trail and water reservoir to your right. Follow this trail. Other trails will appear and intersect. Any trail going up will work. Waterfowl on the bay can be viewed from the shoreline along Highway 19, across from the rest area.*

NANOOSE HILL

N

Stewart Rd

Fairwinds Dr

Northwest Bay Rd

Powder Point Rd

P

Hwy 19

Nanoose Harbour

Dept. of National Defense

movements while soaring, and their V-shaped flight profile, unlike the Bald Eagle's flat profile. Also watch for **Common Raven, Red-tailed Hawk, Cooper's Hawk** and the smaller, multi-coloured **American Kestrel.**

Below the hill, in late February and March when huge schools of Pacific Herring crowd into shallow bays to spawn in the eelgrass, Nanoose Bay can be blanketed with thousands of **Surf, White-winged** and **Black Scoters.** Winter waterfowl abound including **Trumpeter Swans, Common** and **Pacific Loons, Common** and **Barrow's Goldeneye, Horned** and **Western Grebes, American Wigeon, Greater Scaup** and **Bufflehead.**

*On warm days, look for the 20-centimetre-long Northern Alligator Lizard sunning itself on logs or rocks near the edge of the forest.*
*Photo: Jay Patterson*

*The carbohydrate-rich bulbs of Common Camas (left) were an important food source for Native people, who cultivated this wild lily in camas beds on Vancouver Island. Bulbs were harvested during or soon after flowering so they could be distinguished from the extremely poisonous bulbs of the Meadow Death-camas (above), which grows on the same slopes and meadows.*
*Photos: Kim Goldberg*

Fairyslipper orchid. Photo: Trudy Chatwin

# SECTION 3
# West Coast

# Hamilton Swamp

*Peatland marsh with abundant birds*

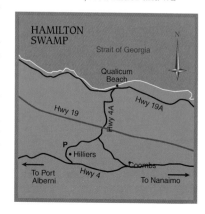

Buckbean. Photo: Kim Goldberg

A short trail through a cedar–alder forest brings you to the edge of a rare **sedge peatland** marsh (also known as Hamilton Swamp) created by beaver damming. From the viewing tower on the shore or the boardwalk extending out into the water you can scan the marsh for **Mallard**, **Pied-billed Grebe** and **Wood Duck**, which all nest here. **Trumpeter Swans** occasionally stop by in the winter. **Ring-necked Duck**, **Hooded Merganser** and **Bufflehead** are common from mid-October through April. The marsh also hosts an extraordinarily high diversity (27 species) of **dragonflies** and **damselflies**. In May and June, the marsh is blanketed with rank-smelling **Buckbean** flowers, which are very attractive to bees, flies and beetles.

The marsh is a popular birdwatching stop for local naturalists who annually sight Vancouver Island's five species of swallows here in the first week in April. **Tree** and **Violet-green Swallows** are expected by that time. But significant numbers of **Cliff**, **Barn** and **Northern Rough-winged Swallows** do not usually arrive on Vancouver Island until the last week of April to May. You may also hear the "*k-dunk*" of the elusive **American Bittern**. **American Robin**, **Song Sparrow** and **Red-winged Blackbird** are common in the **Hardhack**, **Red Alder** and willow thickets along the shore. The denser forest is home to **Winter Wren**, **Chestnut-backed Chickadee** and **Ruby-crowned** and **Golden-crowned Kinglets**. All five of Vancouver Island's **woodpeckers**, including the large

**DIRECTIONS:** *44 km north of Nanaimo on Highway 19, take the Qualicum Beach/Port Alberni turn-off (Highway 4). Proceed toward Port Alberni, and turn right onto Hilliers Road in 1 km. Unmarked parking lot is on left in 1.6 km.*

HAMILTON SWAMP

Strait of Georgia

Qualicum Beach

Hwy 19

Hwy 4A

Hwy 19A

P

Hilliers

Coombs

To Port Alberni

Hwy 4

To Nanaimo

The Red-breasted Sapsucker drills sap wells in trees, which it then revisits to consume the sap and insects—mainly ants—attracted to it.
Photo: Don Cecile

**Pileated**, have been seen or heard here. The **Red-breasted Sapsucker**, and possibly **Northern Flicker**, are nesting.

The **Rough-skinned Newt** (brown on top, orange below) is the least secretive of Vancouver Island's six salamanders and may be seen slowly ambling along the ground near the shore or on the forest trail. If you lift stones or deadfall in search of newts or other salamanders, be sure to replace these objects carefully. Other amphibians found here (with May through August being their most active time) include the **Red-legged Frog**, **Pacific Treefrog** and **Bullfrog**. Bullfrogs are the largest frog in North America, and will eat practically any moving thing they can cram into their ample mouths, including ducklings! Although native to eastern North America, they have been introduced to western regions, including Vancouver Island where they occur from Victoria to Parksville. Bullfrogs can have a devastating effect on native frog species, which they often eat or outcompete. On spring and summer evenings you can't mistake their deep-pitched throaty voices calling for their "*jug o'rum.*" The marsh and surrounding watershed are privately owned and managed by MacMillan Bloedel, but visitors are permitted.

The bumps on the skin of the Rough-skinned Newt are poison glands that can secrete a toxin to deter predators when the newt is severely agitated.
Photo: Kim Goldberg

# Stamp Falls Provincial Park

*Photo: Steve Baillie*

*Salmon and steelhead runs*

Dark-eyed Junco. Photo: BC Environment

Each year more than 500,000 **salmon**, **lamprey** and other fish travel up this important aquatic corridor to spawn in upper Stamp River and Great Central Lake. The Stamp River consistently ranks among the top three rivers on Vancouver Island for angler use and Steelhead catch. From the riverside trail in this forested park you have an excellent vantage point for witnessing the drama of thousands of salmon fighting their way up the falls and fish ladder or circling in a large pool below the falls, collecting their strength for the battle ahead. The **Sockeye** run alone has exceeded 300,000 fish some summers, although 50,000 is more typical. Smaller runs of **Coho**, **Steelhead** and **Chinook** occur here as well from summer into late fall. A portion of the Chinook run is hatchery-reared nearby at Robertson Creek Hatchery.

Look for Sockeye from late June to early September, Chinook from mid-September to mid-November, Coho from mid-August to December, and Steelhead year-round. While Sockeye are the most commercially important fish in the Pacific Northwest, the Chinook (called "Tyee" when it exceeds 14 kilograms) is the largest Pacific salmon. The biggest Tyee on record weighed 57.3 kilograms. Sockeye, by comparison, weigh a mere 2.5 kilograms on average, with a maximum recorded weight of 6.8 kilograms.

When the female Sockeye reaches Great Central Lake, she may lay as many as 4,000 eggs in several "redds," trenches she digs in the gravelly bottom. The male, who has been standing guard,

**DIRECTIONS:** *Take Highway 4 to Port Alberni. Just past town turn right onto Beaver Creek Road at sign for Stamp Falls. Proceed 12.7 km to park entrance. The park contains a small campground.*

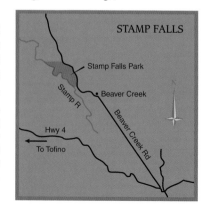

STAMP FALLS

Stamp Falls Park

Stamp R

Beaver Creek

Beaver Creek Rd

Hwy 4

To Tofino

moves in to fertilize the eggs. The female then covers the eggs with gravel, and both adults die. Salmon require cool, clean water and undisturbed gravel to spawn, and the offspring need protective cover. Unfortunately, past logging practices have caused tremendous damage to salmon spawning streams, and logging continues to degrade and eliminate salmon runs despite tougher regulations on the industry.

**Glaucous-winged Gulls** are abundant along the river during salmon runs. Also look for **American Dipper, Bufflehead, Belted Kingfisher, Harlequin Duck** and **Common Merganser** near the falls. As you walk the short trail through a mixed forest of Douglas-fir, Western Redcedar and Bigleaf Maple, look for some of the year-round forest residents including **Chestnut-backed Chickadee, Golden-crowned Kinglet, Varied Thrush, Dark-eyed Junco, Red Squirrel** and **Black-tailed Deer. Black Bears** are drawn to the area during spawning season, so be alert and make noise as you hike the trail. See page 20 for further bear precautions.

*Sockeye Salmon that ascend the falls go on to spawn in Great Central Lake. Photo: BC Environment*

*Since the salmon in Stamp River will spawn farther upstream from your viewing point, they aren't usually in their distinctive spawning colours when they gather in the pools and ascend the falls and ladder.*
*Photo: Steve Baillie*

**BC Parks, Strathcona District:**     250-954-4600

# J.V. Clyne Bird Sanctuary

Photo: Kim Goldberg

*Birds, birds, birds
and butterflies*

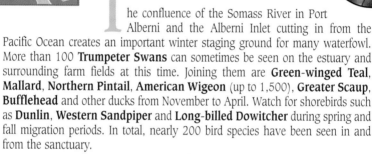

*Northern Rice Root. Photo: Don Cecile*

The confluence of the Somass River in Port Alberni and the Alberni Inlet cutting in from the Pacific Ocean creates an important winter staging ground for many waterfowl. More than 100 **Trumpeter Swans** can sometimes be seen on the estuary and surrounding farm fields at this time. Joining them are **Green-winged Teal**, **Mallard**, **Northern Pintail**, **American Wigeon** (up to 1,500), **Greater Scaup**, **Bufflehead** and other ducks from November to April. Watch for shorebirds such as **Dunlin**, **Western Sandpiper** and **Long-billed Dowitcher** during spring and fall migration periods. In total, nearly 200 bird species have been seen in and from the sanctuary.

From the second yellow gate (see directions), it's a 15-minute walk through a mixed forest to a chainlink fence across the dirt road. The cottonwoods you pass on your right are alive with warblers in spring and fall. **Rough-winged Swallows** and **Belted Kingfishers** nest in the steep sand bank on your left before the fence. Go around the fence (public access is permitted) and follow the gravel laneway beside the huge water pipe. From the higher gangplank along the pipe you can scan the pasture on the opposite side, which can be excellent for Trumpeter Swans in winter. Also watch for **raptors**, including **Short-eared Owl**,

**DIRECTIONS:** *From Highway 4 in Port Alberni, follow signs through town toward Tofino and Ucluelet. After 3 km on River Road, you cross a bridge over the Somass River. Turn left onto Mission Road immediately after bridge and proceed for 1 km to a yellow gate, which is locked weekdays after 4:30 p.m. and weekends. Park and walk (or drive if you can) approximately 1 km on the paved road. (This is a private road on MacMillan Bloedel land, but public access is permitted.) When you see a large-diameter water pipe passing under the road, take the next left onto a dirt road with a yellow gate across it. Walk in to estuary.*

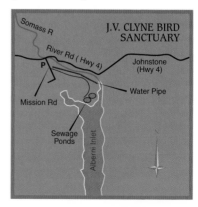

J.V. CLYNE BIRD
SANCTUARY

Somass R

River Rd ( Hwy 4)

P

Johnstone
(Hwy 4)

Water Pipe

Mission Rd

Sewage
Ponds

Alberni Inlet

*Mourning Cloaks overwinter as adults, making them one of the earliest butterflies you will see here in spring. Photo: Don Cecile*

hunting over the pasture. In April and May, hundreds of **Violet-green Swallows** and **Vaux's Swifts** fill the sky.

The laneway takes you past three wastewater ponds, bringing you to a good vantage point for scanning the end of the Alberni Inlet. The first pond (the city's sewage pond) is probably the best location on Vancouver Island to see numerous **Northern Shovelers** in winter—up to 200 on the pond and adjacent marsh. Opposite the third pond (MacMillan Bloedel's effluent pond), you'll pass a tall grove of Sitka Spruce and Western Redcedar on your right where **Bald Eagles** like to perch in winter. The salt marsh contains no fewer than 20 rare plant species including **Wild-flag iris** and **Unalaska Paintbrush**, both of which seldom occur this far south. **Oregon Ash** is also found in the sanctuary, one of very few known sites for this tree in BC. **Northern Rice Root**, also called Black Lily, is dispersed here by small mammals dropping "bulblets" when they feed on the roots. In spring and summer, the sanctuary is adorned with showy butterflies including **Western Tiger Swallowtail**, **Mourning Cloak**, **Painted Lady**, **Western Tailed Blue**, **Spring Azure** and others. The sanctuary is also frequented by **Black-tailed Deer**, **Mink** and a couple of resident **Black Bears**.

*25 percent of the world population of Trumpeter Swans winters on Vancouver Island estuaries and wetlands, including J.V. Clyne. Photo: Don Cecile*

# Broken Group Islands

*Ocean vistas, birds and marine life*

Ruddy Turnstone. Photo: BC Environment

A t the mouth of the Alberni Inlet, opening into the Pacific Ocean, lie more than one hundred rocky islands and islets collectively known as the Broken Group Islands. This forested archipelago dotting the sheltered waters of Barkley Sound is a popular destination for kayakers, canoers, divers and wildlife watchers. The islands have long provided a safe haven for boaters seeking refuge from ruthless storms lashing Vancouver Island's outer coast. Immediately south of the islands lies an infamous stretch of coastline known as the "Graveyard of the Pacific." After a long history of maritime disasters along its shores, a 1906 shipwreck that took 126 lives prompted the construction of a life-saving trail now known as the West Coast Trail. Both the trail and the Broken Islands are part of Pacific Rim National Park, as is Long Beach (page 82). Overnight users of any area of the park must register and pay a fee. There are eight designated camping areas on the Broken Islands.

An excellent way to take in the wildlife and extraordinary scenery of these islands and adjacent waters without an overnight stay is to book a seat on the MV *Lady Rose* or MV *Frances Barkley*, departing from Port Alberni. The two ships are packet freighters delivering mail, cargo and passengers to Ucluelet, Bamfield and other points in Barkley

**DIRECTIONS:** The MV **Lady Rose** and MV **Frances Barkley** depart at 8:00 a.m. from Argyle Pier at the base of Argyle Street in the Alberni Harbour Quay in downtown Port Alberni. Reservations are recommended from mid-June to mid-September. The vessels are operated by Alberni Marine Transportation, which also offers canoe and kayak rentals. Charter cruises can be arranged for groups. Bring warm clothing, binoculars and extra film for your camera. There is a coffee shop on board.

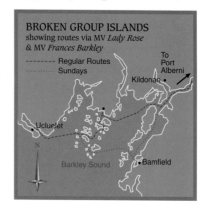

BROKEN GROUP ISLANDS
showing routes via MV *Lady Rose*
& MV *Frances Barkley*

- - - - - Regular Routes
· · · · · · Sundays

To Port Alberni

Kildonan

Ucluelet

Barkley Sound

Bamfield

Photo: Shirley Goldberg

Sound. Both ships cruise down the 60-kilometre-long Alberni Inlet where **Bald Eagles** are commonplace. Watch for **Black Bear** along the shore, searching for crabs beneath rocks.

For best wildlife viewing, select the route and vessel that weaves through the Broken Islands and proceeds to Ucluelet, rather than the route to Bamfield which just skirts the islands. (In 1996, the return fare to Ucluelet was $44.) **Gray Whale** sightings are possible as you near the outer ocean, particularly during their spring migration, which peaks in early April. **Harbor Seal** and **Northern (Steller's) Sea Lion** are common from April to October. Bald Eagles nest throughout the Broken Islands and can be seen any time. Other common birds include **Black Oystercatcher, Great Blue Heron** and **Pelagic Cormorant**. You may see **Mink** and **River Otter** along the shore and **Raccoon**

*Northern (Steller's) Sea Lions at nearby Pachena Point. Photo: Frank Stoney*

and **Black-tailed Deer** on the islands. The shallow and somewhat turbulent waters around the islands receive substantial oxygenation, resulting in increased nutrients, which attract the rest of the food chain: plankton, fish, seabirds and marine mammals. Boaters travelling to this reef-studded area need Canadian Hydrographic Service Charts 3670 and 3671.

*Some 21,000 Gray Whales parade by Vancouver Island's west coast each spring (February to May), many in sight of shore. Photo: Jim Darling*

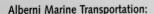

| | |
|---|---|
| **Alberni Marine Transportation:** | 1-800-663-7192 (in season) |
| | 1-250-723-8313 (year-round) |
| **Pacific Rim National Park:** | 1-250-726-7721 |
| **World Wide Web:** | http://fas.sfu.ca/canheritage/ |
| | homepage/parks_hp/natpk_hp/ |
| | pr/pacific_.htm |

# Long Beach

*Photo: Don Cecile*

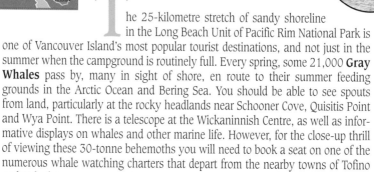

*Gray whales, shorebirds*

*Humpback Whale. Photo: Frank Stoney*

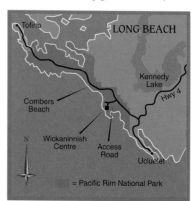

The 25-kilometre stretch of sandy shoreline in the Long Beach Unit of Pacific Rim National Park is one of Vancouver Island's most popular tourist destinations, and not just in the summer when the campground is routinely full. Every spring, some 21,000 **Gray Whales** pass by, many in sight of shore, en route to their summer feeding grounds in the Arctic Ocean and Bering Sea. You should be able to see spouts from land, particularly at the rocky headlands near Schooner Cove, Quisitis Point and Wya Point. There is a telescope at the Wickaninnish Centre, as well as informative displays on whales and other marine life. However, for the close-up thrill of viewing these 30-tonne behemoths you will need to book a seat on one of the numerous whale watching charters that depart from the nearby towns of Tofino and Ucluelet.

If you time your visit for the last two weeks of March or the first week of April you can take in the activities of the annual Pacific Rim Whale Festival. The Gray Whales reach peak numbers here in early April, but as they migrate they are passing by continuously from late February to May. About 40 Grays remain all summer, feeding along the Vancouver Island coast. They rejoin the main herd when it passes by again in late December en route to its calving grounds in Baja California. The whales are moving faster

**DIRECTIONS:** *Long Beach is 286 km northwest of Victoria, via Highway 1 to Nanaimo, then Highway 19 toward Parksville, then Highway 4 to Port Alberni and the west coast. Turn right for Tofino at the Tofino/Ucluelet junction. Wickaninnish Centre turn-off is in 4.8 km. In addition to the Green Point campground at Long Beach, there are several private campgrounds outside the park plus numerous accommodations and amenities in Tofino and Ucluelet.*

on the return journey, led by the pregnant females, and they are not loitering to feed, which makes viewing less reliable, although still possible. The calves are born in the warm Mexican lagoons in January and February, each measuring 4–5 metres at birth and weighing 1 tonne! The whales' 16,000-kilometre round-trip journey (one of the longest migratory circuits of any mammal) begins again in February when the males, juveniles and newly pregnant females head north, followed several weeks later by the cows with calves.

*No other whale besides the Gray Whale is primarily a bottom feeder. Photo: Jim Darling*

In one of nature's many paradoxes, these gargantuan creatures—among the largest on earth—feed on some of the tiniest creatures, including amphipods (in the same family as sand fleas and beach hoppers) and very small shrimp-like plankton. Gray Whales are baleen whales, which means they have no teeth but instead rely on enormous strips of comb-like baleen hanging from the roofs of their mouths to strain millions of tiny creatures from the seawater and mud they sluice through the baleen. When bottom feeding, a Gray Whale rests the side of its head on the sea floor, sucks in a mouthful of sediment and pushes it through its baleen filter with its huge tongue, thereby trapping dinner.

*Rugged coastline at Long Beach. Photo: Kim Goldberg*

Gray Whales were hunted intensely in the previous century, practically eliminating this species from the planet. The Atlantic population disappeared prior to industrial whaling. And the western Pacific population, which spends its summers in Russia's Sea of Okhotsk, numbers only 200–300. Fortunately, the eastern Pacific herd (those you will see at Long Beach) was able to rebuild its numbers from several hundred to the 21,000 or more that exist today after the species received international protection in 1947. In addition to Gray

*Northern (Steller's) Sea Lions gather at a rocky point in the Clayoquot Sound.*
*Photo: Trudy Chatwin*

Whales, **Humpback Whales** (another baleen whale nearly hunted to extinction) are sighted on rare occasions in these waters in the summer and fall when 50–100 are feeding far offshore. **Killer Whales** occur year-round. **Northern (Steller's) Sea Lions** are common along this coast, but some move to inside waters (Georgia Strait) from November to March to feed on Pacific Herring.

Long Beach can be excellent for shorebirds, especially in May. The best birding spot is Comber's Beach (look for the marked turn-off 5.3 kilometres north of turn-off to Wickaninnish Centre). A small stream flows into the ocean here, attracting numerous **gulls** year-round and **Trumpeter Swans** in fall and winter. In May, look for flocks of **Western Sandpiper, Semipalmated Plover, Dunlin** and **Sanderling** on the beach, as well as the occasional **Red Knot** and

*Dunlin in breeding plumage.*
*Photo: Don Cecile*

*The Marbled Murrelet spends its entire life at sea except when it comes ashore to nest in tall trees in coastal rain forests. In 1996, the BC government placed this bird on the provincial Red List of threatened or endangered species due to continued loss of nesting habitat to clearcut logging.*
*Photo: Mark Hobson*

**Marbled Godwit**. **River Otter**, **Black Bear** and, on rare occasions, **Gray Wolf** have all been seen near the stream. Other park mammals include **Mink**, **Raccoon** and **Black-tailed Deer**. Check the rocky headlands at Cox Point and below Wickaninnish Centre for the rock-dwelling shorebirds, primarily **Wandering Tattler**, **Surfbird**, **Black Turnstone** and **Rock Sandpiper**. **Steller's Jay**, BC's official bird, is common throughout the park. Don't forget to look up. Thousands of **Greater White-fronted Geese** and **Canada Geese** fly over these beaches each spring.

*Sanderlings.*
*Photo: BC Environment*

| | |
|---|---|
| **Pacific Rim National Park:** | 250-726-7721 |
| **Ucluelet Visitor Info Centre:** | 250-726-4641 |
| **Tofino Visitor Info Centre:** | 250-725-3414 |
| **World Wide Web:** | http://fas.sfu.ca/canheritage/ homepage/parks_hp/natpk_hp/ pr/pacific_.htm |

# Tofino Flats

*Photo: Don Cecile*

*Seabirds, shorebirds, rare birds*

*Great Blue Heron. Photo: Katherine Ikona*

If you are travelling to Long Beach for bird-watching, you absolutely must include Tofino Flats on your itinerary. This 11-kilometre stretch of tidal mudflats near the village of Tofino is considered the most important waterbird habitat on the west coast of Vancouver Island and among the top ten critical wetlands for migratory water-fowl on the west coast of Canada. More than 200,000 shorebirds alone depend on the flats, particularly during spring migration, at which time **Peregrine Falcons** and **Merlins** can occasionally be seen chasing them. Shorebird numbers peak in late April and early May. Up to 20,000 **Western Sandpiper** have been counted in a single day. Look for **Least Sandpiper** among them. The flats are also excellent for **Whimbrel, Short-billed Dowitcher** and **Semipalmated** and **Black-bellied Plovers.** Such seldom-seen birds as **Marbled Godwit, Long-billed Curlew** and **Red Knot** are all sighted here with some regularity in April and May. The whole Tofino area has long been known as a "vagrant trap" among birders, who will fly across the country to see such rarities as the lone **Falcated Teal** that has been spending its winters on the flats since 1993. Such Asian species that turn up here are presumably channelled along the coast from the Aleutian Islands and stop at the flats because it is a feeding oasis along an otherwise rocky and forested coastline.

The flats, which are covered with a heavy growth of eelgrass and green algae, are also an important migratory stopover and wintering ground for various geese

**DIRECTIONS:** *See Long Beach directions, page 82. Proceed north on Highway 4 toward Tofino. For best access to the flats, turn right onto Sharp Road at the Dolphin Motel, 29 km north of the turn-off to Wickaninnish Centre. Park near hatchery at end. For Grice Bay, turn right onto Grice Bay Road from Highway 4, 12.5 km north of turn-off to Wickaninnish Centre. Park at boat launch at end.*

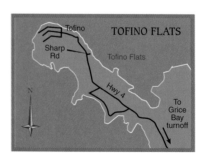

**TOFINO FLATS**

and ducks, including **Brant, Canada Goose, Mallard, Northern Pintail, Gadwall, Northern Shoveler, American Wigeon** and occasionally **Eurasian Wigeon**. Among the diving ducks, you can often see large numbers of **Bufflehead, Greater Scaup, Common** and **Red-breasted Mergansers**, and lesser numbers of **Canvasback** and **Hooded Merganser**. Grice Bay offers a vista of deeper and more open water than the flats, and is good for **Marbled Murrelet** and **Western Grebe**. If you have time, you can hire a boat in Tofino to take you to Cleland Island. Sometimes the whale watching charters will swing by there. Cleland Island is an Ecological Reserve for nesting seabirds including **Pigeon Guillemot, Rhinoceros Auklet, Cassin's Auklet, Black Oystercatcher** and even a few **Tufted Puffins**. You cannot go ashore, but viewing is possible from the water.

## CLELAND ISLAND VIEWING ETHICS:

- View from the water only, using binoculars or spotting scopes.

- Stay well back from the island when birds are nesting.

- Any disturbance may interfere with breeding or cause adults to abandon nests or even kill their young.

- When an adult is spooked off a nest, the eggs or chicks are extremely vulnerable to heat, cold and predation.

*Above: Thousands of Short-billed Dowitchers congregate on the flats each spring. A Dunlin (black belly) stands among them.*
*Photo: Don Cecile*

*Left: Merlin.*
*Photo: BC Environment*

**Tofino Visitor Info Centre:**     250-725-3414

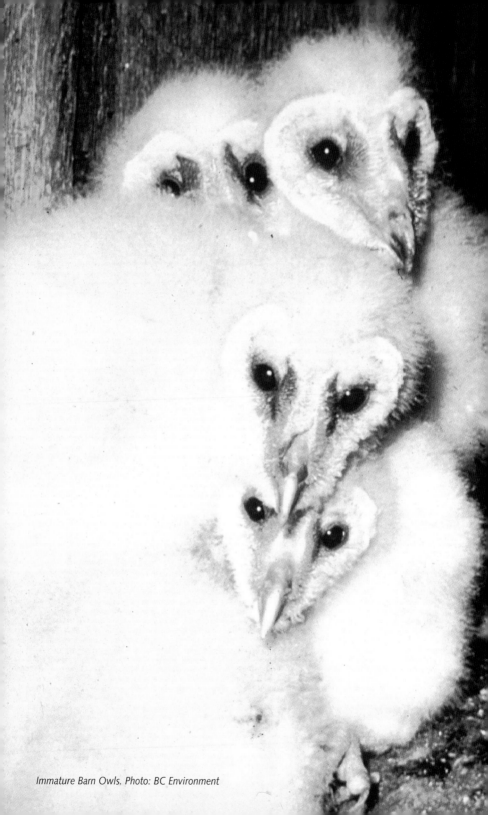

*Immature Barn Owls. Photo: BC Environment*

# SECTION 4
# Parksville/ Courtenay

# Rathtrevor Beach Provincial Park

*Rustic forested viewing trails*

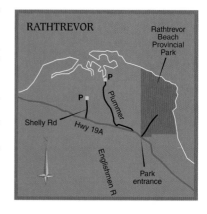

Bonaparte's Gull. Photo: Frank Stoney

Apart from being one of the most popular summer campgrounds on Vancouver Island, Rathtrevor Beach Provincial Park near Parksville supports an interesting diversity of wildlife. The ocean and driftwood zone of the beach, the Douglas-fir forest in the campground, and the marsh and deciduous scrub elsewhere in the park each attract and shelter different species. The forested campground is good **woodpecker** territory throughout the year. Keep an eye out for the showy **Pileated** (Canada's largest woodpecker) with its flaming red topknot, white neckstripe and crow-sized black body. Look for the deep, rectangular holes it jackhammers into cedar trees in its never-ending search for wood-boring insects. Along the marsh trail watch for **Band-tailed Pigeon** (often eating the crimson berries of Arbutus trees in winter), **Northern Flicker** and **Spotted Towhee**. In summer, look for **Common Nighthawk** and **Black Swift** overhead as they snare insects on the wing. Although swifts look like long-winged swallows, they are more closely related to hummingbirds. The nighthawk's closest relatives are the owls.

The beach is one of the best areas to view migrating **Brant** in March and April when thousands of these small sea geese congregate along the shoreline to feed,

**DIRECTIONS:** *Entrance to Rathtrevor is 3 km south of downtown Parksville on coast highway (19A). To view the estuary via the Mine Road trail and tower, turn onto Plummer Road 400 metres north of the Rathtrevor turn-off. Follow Plummer for 1.3 km, park where the road turns right, and take the 5-minute walk down Mine Road and a dirt path out to the tower. To reach the Shelly Road trail and tower, which puts you closer to the ocean, turn right on Shelly Road 600 metres north of Plummer Road. Follow it straight to the end. Park and walk the forest trail out to the estuary and tower.*

RATHTREVOR

Rathtrevor Beach Provincial Park

Shelly Rd

Hwy 19A

Plummer

Englishmen R.

Park entrance

preen, rest and loaf before heading to their Alaskan breeding grounds (see page 92). As you walk north along the beach to the mouth of the Englishman River, look for the small **Bonaparte's Gulls** (black heads in summer) from April through November. Even though the rare sandspit habitat on the Englishman River estuary has been lost to development, the estuary remains an important wintering ground and migratory stopover for numerous waterfowl from September through May. **American Wigeon, Green-winged Teal** and **Mallard** are the most abundant. Also look for **Northern Pintail, Blue-winged Teal, Gadwall** and **Northern Shoveler**. See directions below for access to estuary trails and viewing towers, which are in a Wildlife Management Area but not in the park itself.

*In winter (opposite) or summer (above) plumage, the petite Bonaparte's Gull, with its nasal, chattering voice, is distinctive in any season. Photo: BC Environment*

*Male American Wigeon, also called Baldpate. Photo: Frank Stoney*

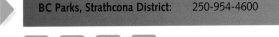

**BC Parks, Strathcona District:**     250-954-4600

# Parksville/ Qualicum Beach

*Photo: Kim Goldberg*

*Stopover for 20,000 Brant geese.*

*Brant. Photo: Kim Goldberg*

I f you have ever felt frustrated or defeated by the inexplicable "sport" of birdwatching in which you can't even be assured of getting a good look at anything with feathers, let alone accurately identifying it, the **Brant** await you—all 20,000 of them. Every spring, immense flocks of these small sea geese (looking something like miniature, dark Canada Geese) descend on the shores of Parksville and Qualicum Beach for their last major food stop before undertaking the final leg of their 10,000-kilometre journey from Mexico to their Alaskan breeding grounds.

The "talking geese," nicknamed for their incessant chattering, begin arriving in the Parksville/Qualicum Beach area in late February and gorge on eelgrass, sea lettuce, green algae and herring roe to build up their fat reserves for the long flight ahead. Their numbers peak in the first 2–3 weeks of April when up to 5,000 Brant can be counted here in a single day, to the delight of their primary predator, the **Bald Eagle**. By early May they're gone. Although the noisy, teeming Brant are quite a spectacle in themselves, the herring spawn in early March attracts thousands of waterfowl (more than 3,000 **Oldsquaw** some years) and **gulls** to the area as well as **Harbor Seals**, **Harbor Porpoises**, and **California** and **Northern Sea Lions**.

In total, 20,000 of the Pacific coast's 140,000 Brant depend on the Parksville/Qualicum Beach shoreline for a vital food and rest stop. Brant wintering grounds in Mexico face constant threat from development. Consequently, this small but increasingly populated strip of Vancouver Island beach is international-

**DIRECTIONS:** *Best Brant viewing locations are: Rathtrevor Beach (page 90); Qualicum Beach (anywhere along public beach and parking area beside highway or from Brant viewing platform 500 metres north of Shady Rest Pub); Brant Point (1.5 km north of Shady Rest Pub turn right on Kinkade Road, then left on McFeely, then left on Surfside).*

*Pacific coast Brant were formerly called Black Brant when they were considered a separate species from east coast Brant. Photo: Frank Stoney*

ly significant for the Pacific subspecies of Brant. Since 1991 an annual Brant festival has been mounted here in early April, drawing several thousand visitors to a three-day nature extravaganza of wildlife art, nature walks and talks, a birding competition, photography workshops, and of course Brant viewing. In 1993, the provincial government declared a 17-kilometre stretch of crucial intertidal foreshore, beaches and estuaries around Parksville and Qualicum Beach a Wildlife Management Area, ensuring this zone's protected status not only for migrating Brant, but for the additional 240 bird species that occur here.

*This adult Golden-haired Flower Longhorn (Cosmosalia chrysocoma), found here, drinks nectar and eats pollen. In larval form it tunnels beneath the bark of oaks, maples, poplars and willows and eats the wood. Photo: Jay Patterson*

**Parksville–Qualicum Beach**
**Tourism Association:** 250-752-2388
**Brant festival information:** 250-248-4117
**World Wide Web:** http://qb.island.net/~bfest/
**E-mail:** bfest@qb.island.net

# Big Qualicum Hatchery

*Photo: Kim Goldberg*

*Woodsy trails, salmon runs*

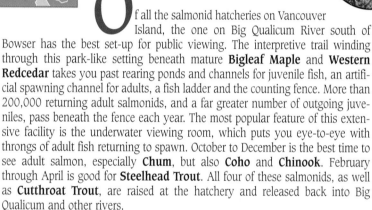

*Varied Thrush. Photo: Frank Stoney*

Of all the salmonid hatcheries on Vancouver Island, the one on Big Qualicum River south of Bowser has the best set-up for public viewing. The interpretive trail winding through this park-like setting beneath mature **Bigleaf Maple** and **Western Redcedar** takes you past rearing ponds and channels for juvenile fish, an artificial spawning channel for adults, a fish ladder and the counting fence. More than 200,000 returning adult salmonids, and a far greater number of outgoing juveniles, pass beneath the fence each year. The most popular feature of this extensive facility is the underwater viewing room, which puts you eye-to-eye with throngs of adult fish returning to spawn. October to December is the best time to see adult salmon, especially **Chum**, but also **Coho** and **Chinook**. February through April is good for **Steelhead Trout**. All four of these salmonids, as well as **Cutthroat Trout**, are raised at the hatchery and released back into Big Qualicum and other rivers.

This hatchery was the first in British Columbia to employ modern innovations for increasing survival rates of eggs and fry. As many as 25,000 Chum spawn in the artificial spawning channel each year and enjoy an egg-to-fry survival rate five times better than that found in nature. By controlling the flow level on the river since 1963, the hatchery has increased the survival rate of juvenile Coho and Steelhead in particular by eliminating the risks of flooding or drying up. While all eggs and fry are susceptible to these risks, young Coho and Steelhead remain in fresh water for one or two years before venturing to sea. With our wild fish stocks dwindling to a fraction of their historic levels, salmonid hatcheries play a vital role in rebuilding these populations.

**DIRECTIONS:** *Hatchery turn-off (signed) is on coast highway (19A), 14.4 km north of Qualicum Beach. Hatchery is open to public year-round from dawn to dusk. Guided tours for groups can be arranged with 2 weeks' notice.*

**BIG QUALICUM HATCHERY**

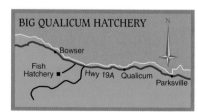

N

Bowser

Fish Hatchery ■

Hwy 19A    Qualicum

Parksville

As you explore the grounds, notice the various forms of predator protection for the fish. The rearing ponds are covered with netting to protect the juveniles from **Belted Kingfisher**, Great Blue Heron and ducks, but you'll likely see kingfishers here anyway. The chainlink fence keeps out Black Bear and Raccoon, although smaller predators such as **Mink**, **Muskrat** and **garter snakes** get through. Along the river itself, **Harlequin Duck** and **American Dipper** are common when fish are spawning. Both birds have the unusual adaptation of being able to walk on the river bottom to forage among rocks for food. **Bald Eagle** and **Osprey** can also be expected at this time.

*Song Sparrows are year-round residents here and elsewhere on Vancouver Island. Photo: D.F. Fraser*

*Bigleaf Maple in spring bloom is one of the best places to look for early returning warblers. Photo: Don Cecile*

**Big Qualicum Hatchery:**    250-757-8412

# Deep Bay & Baynes Sound

Photo: Kim Goldberg

*Abundant bird and marine life*

Stimpson's Sun Star. Photo: Katherine Ikona

For great "armchair" birdwatching, it would be hard to beat Deep Bay where you can often view thousands of gulls, ducks and other seabirds in fall and winter without leaving the heated comfort of your car. Up to 10,000 waterbirds rely on the sheltered and food-laden waters and shoreline of Deep Bay and the adjacent Baynes Sound, which extends north to Comox Harbour. The December arrival and March spawning of immense schools of Pacific Herring create a boisterous feeding frenzy involving not only birds but **Northern** and **California Sea Lions** and **Harbor Seals**. Thousands of **scoters** (**Surf**, **White-winged** and **Black**) blanket Baynes Sound in fall and winter, usually peaking in late October. **Harlequin Ducks** are particularly numerous in November and March. Harlequins dine on mollusks and crustaceans, which are prolific along this shoreline.

The roadside pull-out at Deep Bay offers an excellent view across the channel between the spit and the south end of Denman Island and the Chrome Island lighthouse. In winter, the channel can yield thousands of **Western Grebes** as well as **Horned** and **Red-necked Grebes**, **American Wigeon**, **Marbled Murrelet**, **Common Murre**, **Pigeon Guillemot**, **Common** and **Pacific Loons** and **Oldsquaw**. **Black-bellied Plovers** are common along the shore at the pull-out and throughout this area starting in September. You're also likely to see flocks of **Black Oystercatchers**, **Common Terns** and **Bonaparte's Gulls** at this time. **Black Turnstones** arrive in

**DIRECTIONS** to Deep Bay: Drive 36 km north of Parksville (5.5 km north of Bowser) on the coast highway (19A), and turn right onto Gainsburg Road at the sign for Deep Bay. Keep left at the railway tracks, then right onto Burne Road, and left onto Deep Bay Drive. Park at pull-out on your right, or drive to the beacon light at end.

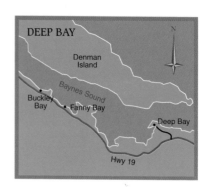

DEEP BAY

Denman Island

Baynes Sound

Buckley Bay

Fanny Bay

Deep Bay

Hwy 19

N

October and reach peak numbers in December and January. Deep Bay's sheltered harbour across the road from the pull-out is also worth checking. You should find **Belted Kingfisher**, **Great Blue Heron** and **Bald Eagle** year-round.

Baynes Sound can be viewed from various points and pull-outs along the coast highway, which hugs the shoreline from Fanny Bay to Union Bay, including the rest stop 3 kilometres north of Buckley Bay. Look for sea lions hauled out on log booms as you drive by the Brico Ship Restaurant at the north end of Fanny Bay and also at Union

Look for Stimpson's Sun Star washed up on beaches after storms. Close-up of underside shows partly extruded stomach with scale worm near base of one arm.
Photo: Katherine Ikona

Bay. The Ship's Point Road turn-off at the south end of Fanny Bay takes you to a small pull-out (at Tozer Road junction) where you can scan the tidal flats for **Greater** and **Lesser Yellowlegs**, **Short-billed** and **Long-billed Dowitchers** and other transient shorebirds during spring and fall migration. Back on the highway, the Hayward Drive turn-off at Royston quickly brings you to Marine Drive, which offers good viewing in fall and winter. **Northern Pintail** is one of the most prominent dabbling ducks here. Watch for **Brant** in March and April. Follow Marine Drive back to the highway, and turn right onto Millard Drive in 2 kilometres for some good viewing at the small park at the end.

Male Northern Pintail stretching.
Photo: Katherine Ikona

# Helliwell Provincial Park

*Cliffside park, birds and sea lions*

Photo: Shirley Goldberg

Pelagic Cormorant. Photo: Trudy Chatwin

The rolling, grassy bluffs of this cliffside park on Hornby Island offer spectacular views of Georgia Strait, which can be teeming with birds and marine mammals during herring season (November to March). Look for **Surf** and **White-winged Scoters**, **Pigeon Guillemot**, **Marbled Murrelet**, the occasional **Ancient Murrelet**, **Pacific** and **Common Loons**, **California** and **Northern (Steller's) Sea Lions** and **Harbor Seal**. Sea lions like to haul out on Flora Island, just offshore from the point. **Bald Eagles** glide by in search of fish, and **Killer Whale** sightings are possible from the high headland. **Pelagic Cormorants** are common year-round and nest on the steep cliffs below the trail, with an occasional **Brandt's Cormorant** perched among them. **Black Oystercatchers** and **Harlequin Ducks** are also present throughout the year.

The loop trail is at least a one-hour walk at a brisk pace. But this alluring site deserves far more time. **Chestnut-backed Chickadee**, **Dark-eyed Junco**, **Golden-crowned Kinglet** and **Winter Wren** inhabit the mature Douglas-fir forest at the beginning of the hike. The bluffs are bordered by quite a different forest of **Shore Pine**, **Arbutus** and **Garry Oak**, and are carpeted with wildflowers in spring, including **Sea Blush**, **Menzies' Larkspur** and **monkeyflower**.

**DIRECTIONS:** *Buckley Bay ferry terminal is 83 km north of Nanaimo on Highway 19. Ask for a Denman/Hornby map at the terminal. Take the hourly ferry to Denman Island, drive 11 km across the island, and catch the connecting ferry to Hornby Island (or spend an hour at nearby Boyle Point Provincial Park and catch the next ferry). Upon disembarking at Hornby follow the main road 8.6 km to a 4-way stop. Turn left onto St. Johns Pt. Road and proceed 4.2 km to the marked turn-off to Helliwell Park.*

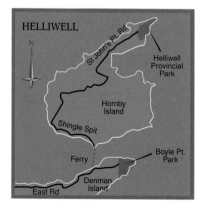

HELLIWELL

St John's Pt. Rd

Helliwell Provincial Park

Hornby Island

Shingle Spit

Ferry

Boyle Pt. Park

Denman Island

East Rd

*Black-tailed Deer (female shown) is found here.*
*Photo: David Nagorsen*

En route to Hornby you can stop at Boyle Point Provincial Park on Denman Island, 2 kilometres beyond the ferry terminal to Hornby. Since the mid-1990s, the majority of sea lions drawn to Georgia Strait in pursuit of Pacific Herring have congregated around the south end of Denman and Hornby islands and in Lambert Channel between the two. The Chrome Island lighthouse, offshore from Boyle Point, should give you a view of them. But there's no telling what part of the strait will be the sea lion hot spot in a few years' time because the herring shift their major staging areas every 5–6 years. The 10-minute ferry rides are mini wildlife watching cruises, taking you through the productive waters of Baynes Sound and Lambert Channel. So don't stay in your car. There is no campground at Helliwell or Boyle Point, but both Hornby and Denman have private campgrounds and other accommodations, and there is limited camping at Fillongley Provincial Park on Denman.

*Sea Blush is a winter annual, germinating in fall and setting seed before summer droughts. Photo: Kim Goldberg*

| | |
|---|---|
| **BC Parks, Strathcona District:** | 250-954-4600 |
| **Denman/Hornby Tourist Services:** | 250-335-2293 |
| **BC Ferries:** | 1-888-223-3779 |
| | (recorded information) |
| **BC Ferries on World Wide Web:** | http://bcferries.bc.ca/ferries |

# Courtenay River Estuary

*Trumpeter swans, waterbirds, seabirds*

*Male Greater Scaup. Photo: Frank Stoney*

With 10 percent of the global population of **Trumpeter Swans** wintering on farm fields near the Courtenay River estuary, this location is considered the single most important wintering site in the world for this elegant bird. Driven close to extinction in the 1930s after years of overhunting, habitat encroachment and a commercial trade in swan skins, Trumpeter Swans rebuilt their global population to today's level of 18,000 after receiving protection in Canada and the US. But their status is still precarious due to development pressures on vital estuaries and wetlands.

Trumpeter Swans are rare breeders in British Columbia, which accounts for their presence on the provincial government's Blue List of species considered vulnerable and at risk. However, they are anything but rare in the Comox Valley where they are a source of considerable aggravation to local farmers whose spring crops are stunted as a result of the swans' winter grazing. Nearly 2,000 swans use this area in winter (November to March), feeding on crop waste, grass and intertidal plants. Organizers of Courtenay's annual Trumpeter Swan Festival, held the first week of February, hope to apply all future profits toward a program to subsidize local farmers who plant winter cover crops on fallow fields to reduce the swans' impact on the productive fields.

**DIRECTIONS.** *Best viewing locations: the viewing blind on Mansfield Drive (turn-off is opposite Driftwood Mall at south end of town, look for binoculars sign on highway); viewing tower on Comox Road (turn right/east immediately after crossing bridge and proceed 1.2 km); Goose Spit Regional Park (continue along Comox Road, then left onto Pritchard, right onto Balmoral, follow it straight onto Hawkins, which leads to parking lot). Swans on fields can usually be seen along Comox Road or Anderton Road.*

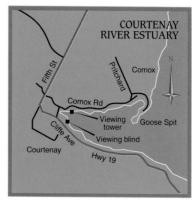

COURTENAY RIVER ESTUARY

Vancouver Island overall supports 25 percent of the world's Trumpeter Swans in winter. Other key estuaries and wetlands on Vancouver Island most heavily used by swans are Cowichan estuary (page 48), Somenos Marsh (page 52) and Nanaimo estuary (page 56).

The Courtenay River estuary offers excellent opportunities for viewing numerous other winter waterbirds and migratory shorebirds. Scan the mudflats for **Greater** and **Lesser Yellowlegs**, **Sanderling**, **Dunlin**, **Short-billed** and **Long-billed Dowitchers** and various **sand-pipers** (**Western**, **Least**, **Semi-**

*Semipalmated Sandpipers (shown) are most often found among flocks of Western and Least Sandpipers. Photo: BC Environment*

palmated, **Spotted**, **Solitary**, **Baird's** and **Pectoral** have all been seen here). Goose Spit on the north bank of the estuary is a good vantage point for viewing wintering ducks and seabirds including **Horned** and **Western Grebes**, **American Wigeon**, **Greater Scaup**, **Oldsquaw**, **Harlequin Duck**, **Bufflehead**, **Surf** and **White-winged Scoters**, **Marbled Murrelet**, **Common** and **Pacific Loons** and many others. The spit is also a stopover point for large

numbers of **Brant geese** on their spring migration to northern breeding grounds. The herring spawn in March draws large numbers of **gulls**, plus **Harbor Seal**, **Osprey** and a profusion of sea ducks. **Mallard**, **Great Blue Heron** and **Bald Eagle** are present year-round on the estuary. Watch for **Peregrine Falcon** hunting over the fields.

*Trumpeter Swans don't metabolize grass as efficiently as their customary cuisine of carbo-hydrate-rich estuary plants. But what the swans lack in efficiency, they regain through continuous grazing—something they can't do on the tidally regulated estuary. Photo: Graeme Fowler*

| Swan Festival: | 250-334-3234 |
| World Wide Web: | http://www.vquest.com/swan/ |
| E-mail: | swan@vquest.com |

# Seal Bay

*Cliffs, wetlands, birds,
rare plants*

Bald Eagle. Photo: Frank Stoney

The network of trails in this 150-hectare woodland park winds through a tall Douglas-fir forest, a rocky seashore and an unusual Hardhack marsh. The ravine trail down to the south beach is a scenic, 30-minute walk through a fir–maple–alder forest high above a steep ravine and then along the ocean cliffs. The dense understory of enormous **Sword Ferns** gives this forest a very primeval feel, although it is actually a naturally regenerated second-growth forest logged between 1913 and 1922. You're likely to hear a chattering **Red Squirrel** or the scolding alarm call of a **Winter Wren** or the high-pitched ringing of **Dark-eyed Juncos** above you in the trees. Down at the seashore, **Harbor Seals** are common throughout the year, but particularly in summer, loafing on rocks that dot the bay. From October through April, look for **Common** and **Pacific Loons, Horned Grebe, Harlequin Duck, Bufflehead, American Wigeon, Surf** and **White-winged Scoters** and **Common Goldeneye. Bald Eagles** are most numerous from January to March. In July 1996, birdwatchers had a thrill when a **Whooper Swan**, a rare Eurasian vagrant that winters in the outer Aleutian Islands, turned up at the beach.

The lagoon loop trail takes you through a slightly more open mixed woodland alongside a creek. After 15 minutes you arrive at the first of two viewpoints onto the **Hardhack** marsh bordered by **Western Redcedar** and **Western White**

**DIRECTIONS:** *From downtown Courtenay, follow main road (Island Highway) north across bridge and turn left. Follow signs to Powell River ferry, turning right on Ryan Road then left on Anderton Road. After 1.4 km on Anderton, turn left to stay on Anderton (don't follow ferry sign). Continue on Anderton (which becomes Waveland) another 4 km, then turn left on Bates Road and continue 1.2 km to parking lot with map and trails to beach. The lagoon trail begins across the road.*

SEAL BAY

P Seal Bay Park

Bates Rd

To Campbell River

Ryan Rd

Anderton

Comox

Courtenay

Hwy 19

Goose Spit

Royston

To Nanaimo

Photo: Kim Goldberg

**Pine.** In the adjacent Crown-owned forest there are three other Hardhack wetlands comprising an even rarer plant community: **Trembling Aspen, Pacific Crab Apple, Hardhack** and **Slough Sedge.** Hardhack wetlands, which occur only in the southeastern lowlands of Vancouver Island and the Gulf Islands, are rapidly disappearing due to agricultural encroachment and other development. Fortunately, the three nearby examples should be fully protected by 1997 when the adjacent forest is scheduled to be added to the existing park. The park expansion may also increase wildlife viewing opportunities, as **Black-tailed Deer, Black Bear, Cougar** and **Barred Owl** have all been seen in the forest.

*Harbor Seal. Photo: Trudy Chatwin*

The loop trail around the marsh can be good for **warblers** in the spring and summer, including **Yellow, Yellow-rumped, Black-throated Gray, Townsend's, MacGillvray's, Wilson's** and **Common Yellowthroat**. If you see a flash of bright yellow and orange in the trees, you may be lucky enough to get a good look at the beautiful male **Western Tanager**. In any season, listen for the nasal "*yank, yank, yank*" of the **Red-breasted Nuthatch,** the most colourful nuthatch and the only one found on Vancouver Island. **Brown Creepers** (also found at this site) creep up tree trunks in a spiral pattern, while nuthatches often walk down head-first. **Song Sparrow, Spotted Towhee** and **Hairy Woodpecker** are present year-round.

*Hardhack. Photo: Kim Goldberg*

*The lovely Chocolate Lily is pollinated by carrion flies and smells like rotting meat! Photo: Frank Stoney*

# SECTION 5
# Campbell River

# Miracle Beach Provincial Park

*Woodsy spot to view woodpeckers*

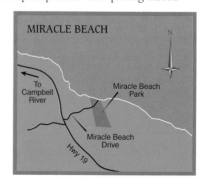

*Raccoon. Photo: BC Environment*

This popular summer park and campground, flanked on the northwest side by the Black Creek estuary, is an exceptionally good spot to see **Pileated Woodpeckers** year-round. Look for the deep rectangular holes these crow-sized birds pound into trees in search of wood-boring insects. The Pileated is by far the largest of Canada's 13 species of woodpeckers, measuring 42 centimetres (16 inches) in length. You may also see Canada's smallest woodpecker, the 17-centimetre **Downy**, here in the park. Other woodpeckers to look for in the second-growth Douglas-fir forest and along the streambank include **Hairy Woodpecker**, **Red-breasted Sapsucker** and **Northern Flicker**. Woodpeckers require forests with standing snags (dead trees) and decaying trees for feeding and nesting. The spectacular Ivory-billed Woodpecker, a larger cousin to the Pileated, is now extinct in North America (except for possibly a few individuals in the pine forests of eastern Cuba) due to logging of the mature swampy forests of the southeastern US since the turn of the century.

In spring and summer, look for **Townsend's** and **Yellow-rumped Warblers** and the beautiful **Western Tanager** (male has bright orange head, yellow body, black wings and tail) in the forest. **Chestnut-backed Chickadee**, **Winter Wren**, **Golden-crowned Kinglet** and **Brown Creeper** are year-round forest residents. Creepers "creep" up tree trunks in a spiral pattern while picking insects and larvae from beneath the bark with their decurved bill. **Western Screech-owl** and **Northern Saw-whet Owl** can be found around the campground at night. **Red Squirrel**, **Black-tailed Deer**, **Raccoon** and occasionally **Black Bear** are also in the park.

MIRACLE BEACH

N

To Campbell River

Miracle Beach Park

Miracle Beach Drive

Hwy 19

• • • • • • • • • • • • • • • • • • • • • • • • • • • • •

*Directions: Park entrance is 23 km north of Courtenay on coast highway.*

The Black Creek estuary, which can be reached by a trail in the park or by walking north on the beach, is a staging area for migrating **Brant geese** in March and April. A few **Caspian Terns** (larger and heftier than the **Common Tern** here in September) can be seen along the beach from May through August. They are evidently non-breeding individuals, as the Caspian Tern's breeding range in Canada is limited to a few localized areas, none on Vancouver Island yet, although their breeding range is moving north. In winter, look for **American Wigeon** and all three species of **scoters** (**Surf**, **White-winged** and **Black**) offshore. Black Creek is also an indicator

*A type of Cuckoo Wasp, found here, so named because it lays eggs in the nests of other wasps, as cuckoo birds do to other birds.*
*Photo: Jay Patterson*

stream for assessing the health of **Coho Salmon** stocks on the east coast of Vancouver Island. You will pass a research counting fence on your left as you drive into the park. Fisheries people are usually on hand during the Coho run from mid-September to mid-November.

*The Pileated Woodpecker keeps its long tongue wrapped around its skull all the way to the top of its head, then shoots it out to snare insects on its barbed and sticky tip.*
*Photo: BC Environment*

**BC Parks, Strathcona District:**    250-337-2400

# Woodhus Slough

*9 different wildlife habitats*

Muskrat. Photo: Trudy Chatwin

This 2-kilometre seaside nature trail located mid-way between Courtenay and Campbell River presents a dramatic example of how wildlife varies with habitat. The first of the nine distinct habitats you encounter is the gravel flats near the trailhead (north end). This area is popular with **House Finch** and **Song Sparrow** (both nesting here) as well as **Brewer's Blackbird**, **American Goldfinch** and, in winter, **Golden-crowned Sparrow**. In summer, **Swainson's Thrush** and **Cedar Waxwing** may be found on the sand plains, which are softly carpeted with moss and reindeer lichen beneath Douglas-fir. Both birds nest in the area.

**Sora** and **Virginia Rail** are present in the marsh in summer, although these secretive birds can be hard to spot. In and around the slough, look for **Beaver**, **Muskrat**, **Great Blue Heron**, **Belted Kingfisher** and **Pacific Treefrog**. **Seacoast Bulrush** is the principal plant in this zone, bathing the marsh and slough in warm golden tones in the fall when it changes colour. The **Cattails** at the south end of the slough are favourite perches for noisy **Red-winged Blackbirds** nesting here in spring and summer. The soft lower stems of the Cattails are a preferred food of the Muskrat, which also uses the long stalks for building its conical lodges, which you may see emerging from the water. In winter, look for Muskrat "runways" in the grass near the sloughbank. Also in winter, **Trumpeter Swans** can be seen on the slough and on the flooded farm fields at the south end of the trail. Joining them are **Canada Geese**, **American Wigeon** and, occasionally, **Cattle Egret**. Of the

**WOODHUS SLOUGH**

Campbell River
Hwy 28  Hwy 19
Salmon Pt
Woodhus Slough Trail
Pub-to-Pub Trail
Oyster R
To Courtenay

*Directions: Drive 27 km north of Courtenay on the coast highway (or 4.3 km north of the park entrance to Miracle Beach) and turn right onto Salmon Point Road at the sign for Salmon Point Resort. Park near restaurant at end and walk back a short distance to trailhead.*

192 bird species seen along this walk, at least 26 have nested in the area including **Merlin, Killdeer, Common Snipe, Green-winged Teal** and **Rufous Hummingbird**.

Locals know this hike as the "pub-to-pub trail" because there is a pub at each end if you continue for another 1–2 kilometres beyond the south end of the Woodhus Slough trail to the Oyster River Nature Park and estuary. The entire pub-to-pub hike takes about an hour each way. Try to pick up the excellent 11-page interpretive brochure, complete with map and bird checklist, called "A Nature Guide to Woodhus Slough through the Seasons." Check for it at the Black Creek Country Market, 2 kilometres south of the entrance to Miracle Beach Provincial Park, or at the Country Junction Market and Deli across the road from the Miracle Beach entrance.

*Male Red-winged Blackbirds are polygamous in rich habitats such as marshes.*
*Photo: Katherine Ikona*

*The Killdeer lays its eggs directly on open ground, usually gravel.*
*Photo: BC Environment*

# Oyster Bay

*Photo: Kim Goldberg*

*Pacific Flyway stop
for birds*

*Juvenile Western Sandpiper.
Photo: Katherine Ikona*

This sheltered bay positioned along the Pacific Flyway (one of the largest bird migration corridors in North America) can be teeming with waterbirds and shorebirds during spring and fall migrations and throughout winter. In fall and winter, look for huge flocks of **Western Grebe** (sometimes thousands) on the bay. **Red-necked Phalarope** and **Common Tern** are seen here in August and September. Non-breeding **Caspian Terns** (larger and heavier than Common Terns) spend their summers along this stretch of coastline, particularly from Miracle Beach to Oyster Bay. In any season you are likely to see **Pigeon Guillemot**, **Common Murre**, **Marbled Murrelet**, **Great Blue Heron** and **Bald Eagle**, although eagles are most numerous in winter. Also look for **Red-throated**, **Pacific** and **Common Loons** year-round. In winter you can expect **Common Goldeneye**, **Bufflehead**, **Common** and **Red-breasted Mergansers** and **Surf**, **White-winged** and **Black Scoters**. At high tide, Surf Scoters have been seen feeding on Common Pacific Littleneck Clams near shore.

The abundant intertidal life in the muddy sediment accounts for the numerous shorebirds often seen feeding here at low tide during spring and fall migration, including **Greater Yellowlegs**, **Western** and **Least Sandpipers**, **Pectoral Sandpiper** (fall), **Long-billed Dowitcher** and occasionally **American Golden-Plover** (September). In winter, **Dunlin**, **Black-bellied Plover** and **Black Turnstone** are common. The bay is partly sheltered by an old causeway and rock breakwater. At low tide you can see remnants of some of the 15 ships that were hauled here and sunk in the 1940s, creating the original breakwater (later

* * * * * * * * * * * * * * * * * * * * * * * * * *

*Directions: Parking lot, trailhead and small rest area are located 30 km north of Courtenay, or 14 km south of Campbell River, on coast highway.*

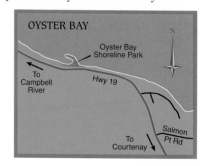

OYSTER BAY

Oyster Bay
Shoreline Park

To
Campbell
River

Hwy 19

To
Courtenay

Salmon
Pt Rd

N

replaced by rocks) to protect log booms in the bay. **Mink** are occasionally seen along the breakwater. **Harbor Seals** routinely use the bay, particularly when the Pacific Herring come in to spawn in late February and early March—an event which also draws numerous diving ducks. **River Otter** are sometimes seen in the bay. **Killer Whale** sightings are possible further offshore. Three kilometres to the north, Shelter Bay is a staging area for migrating **Brant geese** in March and April.

*Greater Yellowlegs are most commonly seen during spring and fall migration, but small numbers overwinter on Vancouver Island. Photo: Don Cecile*

Interesting plants found on the beach plain in the park include **Hooker's Onion**, **Large-headed Sedge**, **Menzies' Larkspur**, **Pale Spring-beauty** and **Seashore Lupine**. Since 1989, local residents have been campaigning for permanent protected status for Oyster Bay Shoreline Park (whose 10-year park-use lease expires in 2002) not only because of its importance to certain species but because a mere 2 percent of this dry maritime subzone of BC's Coastal Western Hemlock biogeoclimatic zone is currently protected.

*Entire-leaved Gumweed, flowering from sticky bracts throughout the summer, is abundant along Vancouver Island's beaches, estuaries and rocky shores, including Oyster Bay.*
*Photo: Kim Goldberg*

# Mitlenatch Island Provincial Marine Park

*Huge seabird nesting colony*

Tiger Lily. Photo: Frank Stoney

Considered "the Galapagos of Georgia Strait" by local naturalists, this arid island located 19 kilometres southeast of Campbell River presents an extraordinary opportunity to observe one of the largest seabird nesting colonies in these waters as well as some spectacular wildflowers. Each year Mitlenatch is used by more than 15,000 adult seabirds and young, the bulk of which are **Glaucous-winged Gulls**. Some 8,000 adult gulls descend on the island in April and May, where approximately half of them breed in huge colonies on the rocky outcrops. Take the nature trail to the bird blind overlooking the colony on the northern end of the island where you can unobtrusively observe nest-building and incubation in May and hatching and feeding in June and July.

Some 1,000 **Pelagic Cormorants** nest high on the cliffs of the south side of the island and should not be disturbed in June and July. Nearly half of the island's 600 **Pigeon Guillemots** are nesting below the cormorants in crevices and small caves or beneath driftwood and boulders. **Black Oystercatcher**, **Northwestern Crow**, **Song Sparrow**, **Barn Swallow** and **Violet-green Swallow** also nest on the island. An additional 151 bird species have been sighted here. Other birds of interest include more than 200 moulting, flightless **Harlequin Ducks** that summer along the shore near Camp Bay and the small flocks of **Rhinoceros Auklet** swimming below the cormorant colony.

From April through August, the island is ablaze with a dazzling succession of wildflowers. **Common Camas**, **Chocolate Lily** and **White Fawn Lily** abound in April and May, followed by **Tiger Lily**,

Directions: Boat charters can be arranged from Campbell River. There is no dock at Mitlenatch, but you can tie up at Camp Bay or anchor at Northwest Bay.

112

Fireweed, Oregon Sunshine, Hooker's Onion, Sea Blush, Harvest Brodiaea and Common Harebell in June and July, and ending with Pearly Everlasting and Spikelike Goldenrod in late July and August. This is also perhaps the most northerly location of Brittle Prickly-pear Cactus due to unique climatic conditions, which give Mitlenatch a near-desert classification. You may see a Wandering Garter Snake (the British Columbia subspecies of Western Terrestrial Garter Snake) around the gull colonies until mid-July, or swimming close to shore in pursuit of sculpins and blennies.

### IMPORTANT

The entire island is very ecologically sensitive throughout the year, but especially during the nesting period of May–August. Never venture off the trails, and do not bring dogs ashore at any time. When adult birds are spooked off their nests, the eggs and chicks become vulnerable to heat, cold and predation by crows and gulls. Even an innocent attempt to get a better picture by leaving the trail may destroy one of the animals or plants of this exceptional park.

*Above: Glaucous-winged Gull and egg.*
*Photo: Steve Baillie*
*Inset photo: Kim Goldberg*

*Left: Pelagic Cormorant colony on cliffs stained white with guano. Photo: Kim Goldberg*

BC Parks, Strathcona District:     250-337-2400

# Discovery Passage & Cape Mudge

*Photo: Kim Goldberg*

*Birds that follow the tides*

*Marbled Murrelet. Photo: Mark Hobson*

If you are in the Campbell River region, you must spend some time scanning the wildlife-rich waters of Discovery Passage. This long, narrow tidal surge channel running between Vancouver Island and Quadra Island is a funnel for migrating waterfowl and attracts all species that follow the tides. Herring season and its prelude (November to March) are particularly prolific, attracting thousands of seabirds, plus **Northern (Steller's) Sea Lions**. Expect large numbers of **Common** and **Pacific Loons, Common Murre, Marbled Murrelet, Pigeon Guillemot, Surf** and **White-winged Scoters, Red-breasted Merganser** and all three **cormorant** species (**Double-crested, Pelagic** and **Brandt's**). **Bald Eagle, Harlequin Duck, Great Blue Heron** and **Harbor Seal** are common year-round. Good viewing can often be had from Discovery Pier, a public fishing wharf located at the south end of Campbell River.

For additional wildlife viewing (as well as some breathtaking ocean vistas), take the 10-minute ferry ride to Quadra Island and proceed to Cape Mudge lighthouse at the island's southern tip where you can hike the grassy bluffs overlooking Discovery Passage and Georgia Strait. The ferry takes you across Discovery Passage, often bringing you in close range of birds and marine mammals that aren't near shore, so have your binoculars handy. At the lighthouse parking lot,

*Directions to lighthouse trail: Ferry to Quadra Island departs hourly from Campbell River. Upon disembarking, follow main road and signs to Cortes ferry and Rebecca Spit until Heriot Bay Road connects with Cape Mudge Road. Turn right onto Cape Mudge Road and proceed 5.5 km to Joyce Road. Turn right onto Joyce, then right onto Lighthouse Road after 1 km. Proceed to parking lot at end, beside lighthouse.*

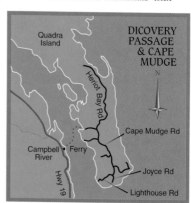

DICOVERY PASSAGE & CAPE MUDGE

Quadra Island

Heriot Bay Rd

Cape Mudge Rd

Campbell River · Ferry

Joyce Rd

Hwy 19

Lighthouse Rd

follow the marked path behind the lighthouse and out along the bluffs in front of Tsa-Kwa-Luten Lodge. Beyond the lodge, take the footpath to the right across the bluffs and down to a cobblestone beach where you can cross a stream by walking on drift logs. A 3- to 5-minute walk along the beach brings you to a steep (but safe) path up a high sand bank covered with **Large-headed Sedge** (also called Mace-head Sedge, due to its sharp, weapon-like flower spike). The grassy clearing at the top affords a spectacular view across Georgia Strait.

*Pigeon Guillemot is the most common breeding alcid on eastern Vancouver Island and the adjacent Gulf Islands. Photo: BC Environment*

In the distance you can see Mitlenatch Island (page 112), which contains one of the largest nesting seabird colonies in the strait. The hike takes 20–25 minutes one-way. But you'll want more time for wildlife viewing. In addition to marine animals, you could see **Black-tailed Deer** in early morning or dusk atop the cliffs or using the sandy path.

*Brandt's Cormorant. Photo: Katherine Ikona*

**BC Ferries:** 1-888-223-3779 (recorded information)

**BC Ferries on World Wide Web:** http://bcferries.bc.ca/ferries

# Rebecca Spit Provincial Marine Park

*Creatures of shoreline and forest*

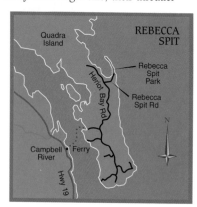

*Male Northern Flicker. Photo: D.F. Fraser*

This narrow hook of land on the east side of Quadra Island offers a surprising variety of wildlife habitats, including a sheltered harbour, a salt marsh, a Douglas-fir forest and a rocky shoreline exposed to the sometimes fierce currents of Georgia Strait. You can drive partway up the middle of the spit. But for best wildlife viewing (and a beautiful hike), park at the first lot and walk the 2-kilometre distance on each side. The Drew Harbour side is one of the few places where **White-winged Scoters** routinely outnumber **Surf Scoters** in winter. Look for other winter ducks and seabirds including **Red-breasted Merganser**, **Common** and **Barrow's Goldeneye**, **Bufflehead**, **Horned** and **Red-necked Grebes**, **Common** and **Pacific Loons**, **Double-crested** and **Pelagic Cormorants** and **Oldsquaw**. **Belted Kingfisher**, **Bald Eagle**, **Great Blue Heron** and **Harlequin Duck** are common year-round.

The forest running down the middle of the spit is bustling with **Winter Wren**, **Dark-eyed Junco**, **Chestnut-backed Chickadee**, **Northwestern Crow**, **Spotted Towhee**, **Song Sparrow**, **Northern Flicker** and **Red Squirrel**. Occasionally a **Common Raven** stops by, prompting dozens of crows to take to the air. Ravens are distinguished from crows by their larger size, their throatier call (not always easy to discern in comparison to Northwestern Crow), their shaggier appearance around the head and throat, and their wedge-shaped tail when flying. A crow's tail ends in a

*Directions: Quadra Island ferry departs hourly from Campbell River, 154 km north of Nanaimo on coast highway. Upon disembarking, proceed straight then follow signs to Rebecca Spit. Rebecca Spit Road turn-off (marked with a BC Parks sign) is 8 km from ferry.*

straight line, not a diamond-like point.

The spit was formed over the centuries as ocean storms battered the nearby cliffs, carrying sand and gravel a short distance offshore and forming Drew Harbour in the process. A 1946 earthquake caused the northern tip of the spit to sink partway into the ocean, killing a grove of trees. Now a salt marsh stands there, awash in pinkish purple in summer when the **Fireweed** blooms. The harbour once sheltered an ancient Native village, abandoned in 1800. To learn more about Quadra Island's Kwagiulth people and their history, visit the Kwagiulth Museum and Cultural Centre at Cape Mudge village on the southern end of the island.

*Horned Grebe in April, changing from winter to summer plumage. Photo: Steve Baillie*

Quadra Island is an easy day trip from Campbell River. The 10-minute ferry ride across Discovery Passage can be excellent for wildlife viewing (page 114). There is sheltered moorage and a boat ramp at Rebecca Spit Park (which is crowded in summer), but no camping. You can camp at the 140-site We Wai Kai campground run by the Cape Mudge Indian Band at the southern edge of the park. There are also various resorts and other accommodations on Quadra. Ask for a map when you buy your ferry ticket.

*Fireweed. Photo: Kim Goldberg*

| | |
|---|---|
| **BC Parks, Strathcona District:** | 250-337-2400 |
| **BC Ferries:** | 1-888-223-3779 |
| | (recorded information) |
| **BC Ferries on World Wide Web:** | http://bcferries.bc.ca/ferries |

# Elk Falls Provincial Park

*Riverside trails, salmon runs*

*Salal berries. Photo: Kim Goldberg*

From the enchanting riverside trail along the Quinsam River in Elk Falls Park you can watch **Chinook**, **Coho**, **Chum** and **Pink Salmon** returning to spawn from September through December. Pinks arrive in August and spawn from mid-September to the beginning of October. Chum spawn in November and December, Chinook from late October to mid-November, and Coho peak in mid-November. Pink, Chinook and Coho Salmon and **Steelhead** and **Cutthroat Trout** are reared at the Quinsam River Hatchery downstream, where the trail ends after a 3-kilometre hike from the campground. Be sure to pick up the interpretive brochure for the trail at the hatchery.

As you walk the trail, notice how the stream habitat is well suited not only for spawning fish but for rearing juvenile salmon and sea-run trout. The shrubs overhanging the bank shade the water, shielding the young fish from heat and predators, primarily **Great Blue Heron** and **Belted Kingfisher**. The young fish also enjoy a food supply as insects fall

**ELK FALLS**
Canyon View Loop Trail

Campbell R

P

P

P

BC Hydro Station

Hwy 28

To the falls

To → Campbell River

**ELK FALLS**
Quinsam River Trail

Campbell R

Hwy 28

Quinsam Campground

Quinsam Rd

Quinsam R

P

Quinsam R Salmon Hatchery

*Directions: At the north end of the town of Campbell River, take Highway 28 toward Gold River and Strathcona Provincial Park. After 1.6 km, take the first turn-off (left) to Elk Falls Park and campground.*

Campbell R

Hwy 28

Hwy 19

Turnoff to Elk Falls & Strathcona Park

into the river from the shrubs. Up-ended root crowns and other large tree debris in the river create good rearing areas for young Coho, Steelhead and Cutthroat. They are also safe resting places for adult Steelhead that winter here before going out to sea via the Campbell River. About 1 kilometre along the trail from the campground you will cross Flintoff Creek, a typical spawning habitat for Coho and a favourite rearing area for all salmon and sea-run trout in the river. Not surprisingly, the Quinsam and Campbell Rivers are very popular with anglers.

*Mink are often seen along stream banks in early morning. Photo: D.F. Fraser*

Near the campground, the trail leads you through a Douglas-fir forest. As the ground gets wetter and lower at the river's edge, notice the abrupt change to **Red Alder** and **Black Cottonwood**. One enormous cottonwood on the trail is at least 2 metres (6 feet) in diameter! A cottonwood this size will transpire thousands of litres of water on a warm summer day. The detour along the old beaver pond via the Kingfisher Trail is worth taking to see some slightly different and more swampy terrain bordered by Douglas-fir. Forest residents include **Chestnut-backed Chickadee**, **Dark-eyed Junco** and **Golden-crowned Kinglet**. Along the river, look for rows of holes high up alder trees drilled by the **Red-breasted Sapsucker** to create permanent sap wells. The sapsucker, a type of woodpecker, revisits these wells to consume the sap and the insects (especially ants) attract-

ed to it. The entire park has an extensive network of trails. The popular Canyon View Loop Trail, beginning across the highway from the campground entrance, at the bridge, takes you across the Campbell River and past two spawning channels where Chinook and Chum are numerous in October and November.

*Townsend's Warbler on Red Alder. Photo: Don Cecile*

**BC Parks, Strathcona District:**     250-337-2400

# STRATHCONA PROVINCIAL PARK:
# Elk River Valley

*Photo: Kim Goldberg*

*Year-round views of Roosevelt elk*

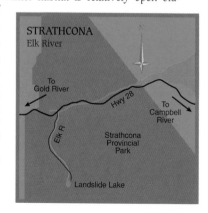

*Great-horned Owl. Photo: BC Environment*

Several hundred **Roosevelt Elk** spend a portion of each year inside the park, and 40–50 of them regularly winter in the Elk River Valley at the park's north end. You're most likely to see winter herds in the valley from late November until early March when they move to higher elevations for their spring and summer grazing. Some 15–20 elk remain in the valley year-round, so elk sightings are always possible. The popular Elk River Trail, a 10-kilometre hike one-way, follows age-old paths worn by elk moving from their sub-alpine summer range to the lush and unlogged valley each winter. Lower reaches of the Elk River Valley along Highway 28 have been logged, but the trail takes you through pristine forest along the west bank of the Elk River. The trail is a minimal climb (550-metre elevation change), and there are designated camping areas along the way.

For a shorter hike through elk territory, take the 400-metre Elk River viewing trail. It follows a powerline cut through a boggy area beside the Elk River, ending at a viewpoint overlooking the river and a hillside. Elk are typically seen grazing on hillsides, in meadows and other natural openings, so keep an eye on your surroundings while you're driving. It's possible to see elk anywhere along the road to Gold River. Their favourite winter habitat is relatively open old-growth forest with an abundance of huckleberry, elderberry or Devil's Club.

• • • • • • • • • • • • • • • • • • • • • • • • • • • • • • • • • • •

*Directions: Highway 28 to Strathcona Park begins at the north end of Campbell River, 157 km north of Nanaimo on Highway 19. Park entrance is in 47 km. At the junction 1.3 km beyond the entrance, stay on Highway 28 (to Gold River). Turn-off to short Elk River viewing trail (marked with binoculars sign) is on right, 21 km beyond park entrance. Trailhead for the major Elk River Trail is in another 5 km.*

STRATHCONA
Elk River

To Gold River

Hwy 28

To Campbell River

Elk R

Strathcona Provincial Park

Landslide Lake

Vancouver Island's other large mammals—**Black Bear**, **Gray Wolf**, **Cougar** and **Black-tailed Deer**—are also present in Strathcona Park and could be encountered anywhere, although bear and deer are more likely to be seen in the Thelwood Creek area (page 122).

Established in 1911, Strathcona is British Columbia's oldest provincial park and the largest on Vancouver Island, covering more than 210,000 hectares of rugged mountain wilderness and valleys. It contains one of the highest waterfalls in Canada (Della Falls with a 440-metre drop) and the tallest mountain on Vancouver Island (the Golden Hinde with a 2,200-metre summit). There are two drive-in campgrounds in the park and various hike-in campsites. There is also the privately run Strathcona Park Lodge, 4.5 kilometres before the park entrance via Highway 28. Gas up in Campbell River. There is no gas in the park or en route.

*Gray Wolf. Photo: Mark Hobson*

*Roosevelt Elk are larger and darker than Rocky Mountain Elk, the other elk subspecies found in British Columbia. The antlers of the male Roosevelt curve inward, allowing him easier passage through dense coastal forests.*
*Photo: Mark Hobson*

**BC Parks, Strathcona District:**   250-337-2400

# STRATCHONA PROVINCIAL PARK:
# Thelwood Creek

*Photo: Kim Goldberg*

*Bear, deer, swans and mountains*

*Pacific Bleeding Heart. Photo: Kim Goldberg*

One of the best wildlife viewing areas in this huge, mountainous park is the Thelwood Creek Valley at the south end of Buttle Lake. This is perhaps the best location in the park for spotting **Black-tailed Deer**, **Beaver**, **Black Bear**, **Trumpeter Swan** and a variety of other birds. For best viewing of the Thelwood Creek floodplain and sedge meadows, walk or drive along Jim Mitchell Lake Road, which flanks the west side of the creek. Spring and early summer are the best times for seeing deer or bear here. Deer are most active in mornings, evenings or moonlit nights. Never try to approach or feed bears. Read the bear and cougar precautions on page 20 for further advice. **Marten**, **Mink** and occasionally **Gray Wolf** are also seen here. Watch for **Merlin** and **American Kestrel** hunting over the meadows in summer.

The nearby Price Creek Trail takes you through a Red Alder forest (grown since a 1958 fire) along the Thelwood Creek Valley and past an active beaver pond with a beaver lodge and dams. Near the water, **Bald Eagle**, **Kingfisher** and **Great Blue Heron** are likely year-round. **Pied-billed Grebe**, **Mallard**, **Green-winged Teal** and **Red-winged Blackbird** can be expected in summer. The forest contains **Hairy** and **Downy Woodpeckers**, **Northern Flicker**, **Steller's Jay** and **Varied Thrush** in any season. For your best chance of viewing **White-**

• • • • • • • • • • • • • • • • • • • • • • • • • • • • •

*Directions: See page 120. At the junction 1.3 km beyond the park entrance, proceed south down Buttle Lake instead of turning right for Gold River. Marked parking lot for Flower Ridge Trail is 30 km beyond junction, near south end of Buttle Lake. Marked turn-off for Price Creek Trail is 5 km beyond Flower Ridge Trail, at southern tip of Buttle Lake. Jim Mitchell Lake Road turn-off is 300 metres beyond Price Creek turn-off.*

tailed **Ptarmigan** (and possibly **Three-toed Woodpecker** if you are exceptionally lucky), take the Flower Ridge Trail, which leads steeply up to the alpine tundra, gaining 1,250 metres of elevation over its 6-kilometre length.

You can't help but notice the numerous shoreline stumps as you drive down Buttle Lake. The lakeshore forests of Buttle and Upper Campbell Lakes were clearcut in 1956 prior to the water level being raised to create a reservoir for a major BC Hydro power generating station. A fire two years later charred the stumps and burned approximately 2,000 hectares in the Thelwood Creek Valley. The

*Few predators other than garter snakes can tolerate the bitter, numbing poison secreted from the warts and parotoid glands of the Western Toad, found here. Photo: BC Environment*

increased water level in Buttle Lake and at the mouth of Thelwood Creek reduced the winter range for Roosevelt Elk here. Only a few elk still reside in this part of the park and are unlikely to be seen. The raised water level also caused the wintering **Trumpeter Swans** to disperse to smaller lakes and sloughs, although a few can usually be found at the south end of Buttle Lake, across the road from the mouth of Thelwood Creek. Because of the size of this park and the variety of trails, you should pick up a map from BC Parks or a tourist bureau before you head in.

*Black-tailed Deer (male shown) was once considered a distinct species, but is now classified as the northwest Pacific coast sub-species of Mule Deer. Photo: D.F. Fraser*

**BC Parks, Strathcona District:**    250-954-4600

# Menzies Elk Demonstration Forest

*Photo: D.E. Fraser*

*Driving tour of bear, deer, elk*

*Skunk Cabbage. Photo: Kim Goldberg*

This 47-kilometre loop drive on an active logging road takes you past a variety of elk habitats in a managed second-growth forest. A herd of approximately 100 **Roosevelt Elk** winter in this area. You will need to pick up the map and brochure titled "Elk Habitat Management: A Self-Guided Wildlife-Forestry Interpretive Car Tour" from the Ministry of Forests office in Campbell River (370 S. Dogwood Street) to know where you're going and what you're looking at. Your best bet for viewing elk is late fall and winter along Snowden Road between stops #6 and #7. Other large mammals to watch for include **Black-tailed Deer**, **Black Bear** and, occasionally, **Cougar**. **Bald Eagle**, **Osprey** (near lakes), **Common Raven** and **Steller's Jay** are fairly common. The Menzies Mainline is in good condition, and the Mary's Lake Road turn-off to stop #1 is the worst road you'll encounter.

In the previous century, elk were widespread in central and western North America. But they were also a big game favourite of early settlers and soon disappeared from 90 percent of their original range. Roosevelt Elk, the subspecies found on Vancouver Island, once ranged from San Francisco to southwestern BC. Today, BC's population of this subspecies is limited to about 3,000 animals mostly on northern Vancouver Island. Recent transplants from the island have re-introduced Roosevelt Elk to southern BC's coastal mainland (Sechelt Peninsula and Powell River).

Some 400 elk live here in the Sayward Forest in several small non-migratory

*Directions: Approximately 14 km north of Campbell River on Highway 19, turn west onto the Menzies Mainline logging road at the large sign for MacMillan Bloedel's Menzies Bay Division. (This is also the route to Morton Lake Provincial Park campground, which is about 18 km in.) Entire driving tour is a 3.5-hour round trip from Campbell River.*

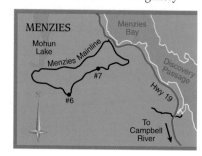

*The larvae of the Golden Buprestid beetle tunnel into and feed on dead and dying Douglas-fir and other conifers. Larvae have been known to live for as long as 75 years in some logs.*
*Photo: Jay Patterson*

herds and two large migratory herds. Important elk forage species found along the driving tour include **Dull Oregon-grape, Red Huckleberry, Salmonberry, Twinflower, Sword Fern, Deer Fern, Devil's Club, Skunk Cabbage** and **Western Hemlock** seedlings. Clearcut logging can adversely affect elk herds by eliminating the forest cover they require for security from predators and humans, for protection from temperature extremes, and for relief from deep snow which limits their access to food.

Each year male elk shed their antlers in March and April and grow new racks in time for the rutting season, beginning in September, when bulls spar with each other for control of a harem of cows. Their "bugling," a sound that has become emblematic of wilderness itself, can be heard at this time. The white-spotted calves are born the following year in late May or early June.

*Douglas-fir, which can reach a height of 76 metres (250 feet), has historically been the most economically important tree species on Vancouver Island. Its cones are distinguished by the three-pronged bracts extending beyond the scales. Photo: Kim Goldberg*

**Ministry of Forests, Campbell River District:**     250-286-9300

125

# Ripple Rock Trail

*Windy ocean bluff, seabirds*

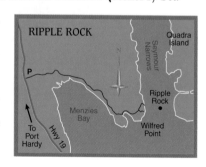

Ladies' Tresses. Photo: Kim Goldberg

After claiming more than 100 lives in dozens of shipwrecks, the dangerous underwater pinnacles for which this trail is named were blown out of the water in 1958 with the largest non-nuclear explosion in history. The trail just north of Campbell River takes you through a mixed Douglas-fir forest along Menzies Bay and out onto a windy bluff high above Seymour Narrows. Here you can gaze across the sometimes roiling waters that used to conceal the notorious Ripple Rock a mere 1.8 metres below the surface at low tide.

The first leg of the trail along the powerline cut offers good birdwatching opportunities for forest and hedgerow species including **Downy** and **Hairy Woodpeckers** and **Varied Thrush** (a "dressed up" robin with dark breast band and orange markings on wings and head). In summer, look for **Orange-crowned** and **Townsend's Warblers**. Be sure to take the short walk out to Menzies Bay at the end of this first leg, where you'll find an assortment of ducks, gulls and shorebirds during spring and fall migration. Even in summer, a relatively "dead time" for seabirds, Menzies Bay should yield **Pigeon Guillemot**, **Belted Kingfisher**, **Bonaparte's Gull**, **Glaucous-winged Gull**, **Killdeer** and **Great Blue Heron**. **Harbor Seal** is common year-round.

From the Wilfred Point lookout over Seymour Narrows—if you're patient, lucky and have a good pair of binoculars—you could see **Northern (Steller's) Sea Lion** in spring and **Harbor Porpoise**, **Dall's Porpoise** or **Killer Whale** any time. In the shady forest of prime Douglas-fir and Bigleaf Maple, look and listen for **Pileated Woodpecker** and **Red Squirrel**. The squirrels are responsi-

**RIPPLE ROCK**

Quadra Island

Seymour Narrows

P

Ripple Rock •

Menzies Bay

Wilfred Point

To Port Hardy

Hwy 19

*Directions: Parking lot and small sign are approximately 16 km north of Campbell River on Highway 19, on the right-hand (east) side.*

*Ripple Rock trail. Photo: Kim Goldberg*

ble for the "cone cobs" (fir cones with all the bracts and scales chewed off) you see on the ground. There are also some fascinating plants along the way. The ghostly white **Indian-pipe**, which feeds off nearby conifers via underground fungi, is surprisingly plentiful along the forest trail. At the Wilfred Point lookout don't miss the numerous **Ladies' Tresses orchids** scattered across the rocky bluff, blooming in July and August with spiral spikes of delicate white flowers.

The trail contains some steep grades, particularly the short climb up the rocky bluff at the end for the viewpoint. But families with children do traverse it. Expect to spend two to three hours on this 8-kilometre round trip. Map and brochure are available from the Ministry of Forests office in Campbell River (370 S. Dogwood Street).

*The Clouded Salamander, found here, is mainly nocturnal and will climb high up trees in damp, mossy Douglas-fir forests. This species occurs on Vancouver Island and in Oregon but, oddly, not in Washington or mainland BC. Photo: Jay Patterson*

**Ministry of Forests, Campbell River Division:** 250-286-9300

Hoomak Lake. Photo: Shirley Goldberg

# SECTION 6
# North Island

# Salmon River Estuary

*Whales, winter waterbirds*

*Osprey. Photo: Don Cecile*

Bordering the village of Sayward on Johnstone Strait, the mouth of the Salmon River may be Vancouver Island's most important estuary habitat for winter waterfowl north of Courtenay/Comox. The remainder of the island's northeast coastline is mostly steep and rocky. At one time this estuary sheltered and sustained the island's largest wintering population of **Trumpeter Swans**, which are still numerous here. Fall and winter are the best times to visit the 52-hectare Salmon River Wildlife Reserve. In addition to the majestic swans, expect large numbers of dabbling ducks—mainly **Mallard**, **Northern Pintail**, **American Wigeon** and **Green-winged Teal**. **Lyngby's Sedge** borders the shoreline throughout the estuary and is a principal food source for the dabblers and swans in early spring due to its high protein content. **Bufflehead** and gulls are also abundant. The small **Bonaparte's Gull** is the most prevalent gull in summer and fall. **Mew**, **Herring** and **Glaucous-winged Gulls** are present throughout the year, as is **Bald Eagle**, **Belted Kingfisher** and **Great Blue Heron**. Look for the statuesque outline of the heron in channels and pools where it waits patiently for sculpins and other small fish to swim into striking range. In addition to eagles, other raptors that have been seen fishing or hunting over the estuary include **Osprey**, **Red-tailed Hawk**, **Merlin**, **American Kestrel** and **Sharp-shinned Hawk**.

The Kelsey Bay wharf at the end of the road gives you a view of the outer estuary where **Harbor**

*Directions: Drive 47 km north of Campbell River on Highway 19 and turn right at the Sayward junction. Proceed 10 km to Sayward's "Welcome" sign. Turn right immediately after the sign, cross MacMillan Bloedel's access road, continue straight for about 500 metres, and park when the gravel road turns left. Walk the rest of the road and trail out onto the estuary. You can also scan the estuary from the two pull-outs on MB's access road. To reach the Kelsey Bay wharf, continue straight past the welcome sign for another 2 km.*

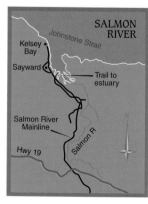

SALMON RIVER

Johnstone Strait

Kelsey Bay

Sayward

Trail to estuary

Salmon River Mainline

Hwy 19

Salmon R

*1996 was an invasion year for Snowy Owls on Vancouver Island when a drop in the lemming population on the Arctic tundra forced the owls south in search of food.*
*Photo: Frank Stoney*

**Seals** are often seen. Keep an eye out for the tall, black dorsal fins or "blow" of **Killer Whales**, which live in Johnstone Strait (page 134). Whale watching charters depart from Kelsey Bay. The estuary is also used by **Black Bear, Raccoon, River Otter** and **Black-tailed Deer** (our coastal subspecies of Mule Deer). Look for deer on the east-side flats on summer evenings or mornings. They sometimes wander through "downtown" Sayward.

*Look for Short-billed Dowitchers here in October.*
*Photo: Don Cecile*

# Sayward to Port McNeill Highway

*Bear, deer and
elk country*

*Northwestern Salamander. Photo: Jay Patterson*

Few people will make the scenic drive from Sayward to Port McNeill on northeastern Vancouver Island without seeing at least one large mammal alongside the road or ambling into the forest. **Black-tailed Deer, Roosevelt Elk** and **Black Bear** are common year-round. **Cougar** and **Gray Wolf** are also present but are less frequently spotted. Just before the start of this run through wilder and more remote country, be sure to check the farm fields on the south side of Highway 19, 1 or 2 kilometres before the Sayward junction, where a resident elk herd (with calves in summer) is sometimes found grazing.

Your best viewing along the route is usually right from your vehicle while driving, since there is no telling exactly where large mammals may be. The highway creates a momentary barrier for them in their travels, which is why you are more likely to see them from your car than from a designated viewpoint. However, there are numerous pull-outs and several rest stops along the way, the most interesting being the Hoomak Lake rest area about 75 kilometres beyond the Sayward junction, and shortly before the Woss turn-off.

Hoomak Lake is home to **River Otter** and **Beaver**, whose gnawed trees are visible along the shore, and it has been stocked with **Cutthroat Trout**. It is also a stopover for **Trumpeter Swans** and various ducks in the late fall and winter. **Steller's Jay, Dark-eyed Junco, Red-breasted Sapsucker** and **Chestnut-backed Chickadee** are common forest residents year-round. Be sure to take the well-signed interpretive trail through the forest and along the lakeshore, which identifies all the trees and various other species. The trail is an old railway grade (with the rails long since removed) dating back to the 1930s when logs were hauled by steam locomotives. Watch for

SAYWARD to PORT McNEILL

Port McNeill · · · · · Sayward

Woss · Hwy 19

Hoomak · Crowman
Lake · Lake

Pacific Ocean

elk foraging in the wetlands just before Crowman Lake (about 5 kilometres before the Hoomak Lake rest area), and also 3 kilometres north of Woss near the highways yard.

When hiking through areas used by large predators, it is always advisable to make noise by talking, singing, whistling or wearing a bell on a backpack, so they know you are coming and aren't startled by an unexpected confrontation. Predators will generally avoid you if given the chance. However, after emerging from hibernation in the spring, bears are concentrating on foraging and are sometimes unaware of peo-

*The Black Bear is the largest predator on Vancouver Island, and can weigh more than 200 kilograms.*
*Photo: Mark Hobson*

ple. Read the bear and cougar precautions on page 20 for further advice. A recreation map of the area is available from the BC Forest Service.

*Cougar.*
*Photo:*
*D.F. Fraser*

**BC Forest Service, Port McNeill District:** 250-956-5000

# Johnstone Strait & Blackfish Sound

*Best place to see killer whales.*

Common Loon. Photo: Frank Stoney

These sheltered waters along Vancouver Island's northeast coast are probably the best place on the entire west coast of North America to view **Killer Whales**, also known as "orca" and "blackfish." Up to 200 whales routinely travel through this area in summer and fall in search of migrating salmon and other fish. Killer Whales are the largest member of the dolphin family, with the adult male reaching a weight of nearly 10 tonnes. Be alert for sprays of waters or "blow" revealing a family group or "pod" travelling beneath the surface. You may also see their tall, dark dorsal fins slicing through the water. If you're especially lucky, you could witness one of these spectacular creatures leap from the water or "breach." Killer Whales inhabit every ocean of the world. More than 300 known as "residents" are found along the coast of BC and Washington state. An additional 200 known as "transients," and another 200 known as "offshore," also occur along the same stretch of coastline.

The Robson Bight (Michael Bigg) Ecological Reserve, near the mouth of the Tsitika River in Johnstone Strait, is world famous for its rubbing beaches where Killer Whales come to rub their sleek bodies on the smooth, dark pebbles near shore. The reasons for this behaviour are unknown, although theories among researchers range from skin hygiene to "it feels good." The reserve is closed to the public so that the whales can have a place to feed, rest and rub themselves on the beaches, free from human disturbance. With some 30,000 people coming

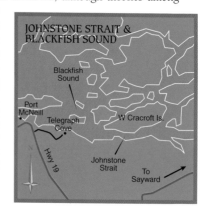

JOHNSTONE STRAIT & BLACKFISH SOUND

Blackfish Sound

Port McNeill

Telegraph Cove

W Cracroft Is.

Johnstone Strait

To Sayward

Hwy 19

*Directions: Whale watching charters depart from Sayward/Kelsey Bay, Telegraph Cove and Port McNeill (all north of Campbell River off Highway 19), and from Alert Bay on Cormorant Island, reached by ferry from Port McNeill.*

to the area in 1994 to view whales, and 100,000 whale-watchers predicted for the year 2000, it is imperative that private boaters respect the boundaries of the sanctuary. The federal government's current practice of allowing commercial fish boats in the sanctuary while whales are present is a contentious issue among pleasure craft owners and conservationists.

Whales in the sanctuary can be viewed from outside the boundary, and there are usually other good viewing opportunities throughout Johnstone Strait and Blackfish Sound. Charter boat operators often rely

## WHALE-WATCHING ETHICS:

- Never chase or split up a pod; travel parallel to the whales and at their speed

- Travel slowly (4 knots) when close

- Don't move in closer than 100 metres; minimize the time you spend travelling with them

on a system of radio communication to locate pods of whales. Some charter boats are equipped with hydrophones (underwater microphones) so you can hear the whales' vocalizations. Researchers have identified many distinct sounds made by Killer Whales, ranging from bursts of sonar-like clicks they emit to navigate and echo-locate prey, to communication sounds such as squeaks, whistles and shrill calls directed to other members of their pod. Each pod has its own distinct dialect. Other marine mammals you may see in these waters include **Harbor Seal, Northern (Steller's) Sea Lion, Dall's Porpoise, Harbor Porpoise, Pacific White-sided Dolphin** and **Minke Whale.**

*Killer Whale breaching.*
*Photo: Frank Stoney*

| Sayward Tourist Information Centre: | 250-282-3265 |
| Port McNeill Tourist Information Centre: | 250-956-3131 |
| Alert Bay Infocentre: | 250-974-5213 |

# Alert Bay

*"Drowned forest" on a remote island*

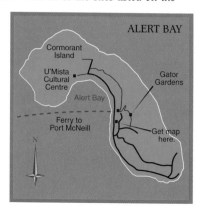

Bald Eagle. Photo: Don Cecile

Aside from the fact that Alert Bay is one of the most charming and historically fascinating towns to spend a day exploring, the ferry ride over from Port McNeill can be quite productive for gulls, ducks, alcids and marine mammals. And an unusual ecological park awaits you at the end of the ride. From the ferry, scan for **Pigeon Guillemot**, **Marbled Murrelet**, **Common Murre**, **Oldsquaw**, **Red-necked** and **Western Grebes**, **scoters** and **loons**. **Bonaparte's**, **California** and **Mew Gulls** are common in late summer. **Glaucous-winged** and **Ring-billed Gulls** are seen year-round. Look for **Black Turnstones** near the dock on the Port McNeill side, where **Bald Eagles** commonly perch on the pilings. **River Otter** are sometimes seen near the shore. **Harbor Seal**, **Pacific White-sided Dolphin** and **Killer Whale** are all possible sightings during your crossing, particularly from early July to mid-October. Many whale watching charters depart from this region.

Upon arriving at Alert Bay on Cormorant Island, your first stop should be the Infocentre (turn right as you disembark). Here you can pick up the Gator Gardens map and plant brochure before heading up the hill. Many tourists leave their cars in Port McNeill since the entire island is less than 5 kilometres long and barely 1 kilometre wide (but hilly). But if you want to visit all of the sites listed on the

"Guide to Historic Alert Bay" brochure in one day, a car or bike would be advisable. For information on traditional uses of local plants, visit the native plant garden and indoor display at the U'Mista Cultural Centre in Alert Bay.

Gator Gardens itself is not particularly rich in animal life, and if you come

*Directions: From Campbell River, drive 196 km north on Highway 19 to Port McNeill and take the 45-minute ferry ride to Alert Bay.*

**ALERT BAY**

Cormorant Island

U'Mista Cultural Centre

Alert Bay

Gator Gardens

Ferry to Port McNeill

Get map here.

*The Western Screech-owl hunts soon after dusk, never far from trees. Photo: BC Environment*

expecting alligators, you're in for a disappointment. But from the boardwalk trail winding through this eerily beautiful drowned forest you should see **Common Ravens** and **Bald Eagles** keeping watch from atop the cedar snags delicately draped in the ghostly green **Common Witches' Hair** lichen. **Violet-green Swallows** nest in the cedars in spring and summer. **Western Screech-owls** are occasionally seen or heard. You may also see **Song Sparrow**, **Belted Kingfisher**, **Downy Woodpecker**, **Varied Thrush**, and in spring, **Hooded Merganser**. Named for its Everglades-like appearance (where alligators do abound), this natural swamp is fed by an underground spring that backed up more than a century ago, killing the surrounding trees, when it was dammed to obtain fresh water for a fish saltery.

*Look for culturally modified cedar trees bordering the swamp. Historically, Native people harvested strips of bark without killing the trees to make hats, baskets, twine and rope. Photo: Kim Goldberg*

BC Ferries (Port McNeill):            250-956-4533
BC Ferries (24-hour information):     1-888-223-3779
BC Ferries on World Wide Web:         http://bcferries.bc.ca/ferries
Alert Bay Infocentre:                 250-974-5213

# Cluxewe Salt Marsh & Estuary

*Dabblers, divers, eagles, bears*

Photo: Kim Goldberg

Female Red-breasted Merganser.
Photo: D.F. Fraser

This important north Island wintering ground and migratory stopover for geese, ducks and other waterfowl is unique on Vancouver Island. Although the salt marsh is quite close to the estuary, it is isolated from freshwater flows. When you explore the region, notice how different species prefer one habitat over the other. The dabbling ducks (predominantly **Green-winged Teal**, **Mallard** and **Northern Pintail**) favour the salt marsh, as do the **Canada Geese**. The diving ducks (mainly **Bufflehead**, **Surf Scoter** and **Harlequin Duck**) as well as **Brant** and **Trumpeter Swans** are more commonly seen in the estuary. Up to 100 swans are here in winter. Brant are most numerous in early to mid-May. **Bald Eagles** can be seen year-round, mainly in the forest zone, but particularly in October and November when they come to feast on spawned-out carcasses of Pink, Coho and Chum Salmon. **Black Bears** feed in the sedge/grasslands throughout the estuary and salt marsh.

Estuaries (places where rivers flow into the sea) are crucial to the survival of winter waterfowl. Brackish estuaries and salt marshes are often the only available bodies of water that don't freeze over, providing accessible food when the temperature drops. Waterfowl wintering on ponds, lakes and flooded fields will all turn up on the nearest estuary during a cold snap. Estuaries that aren't current-

*Directions to salt marsh: On Highway 19 drive 14 km northwest of the Port McNeill turn-off, then turn right onto the Misty Main logging road. Proceed 800 metres until it ends at a junction with a larger logging road. Turn right, drive 1 km and take the first road to your left. Proceed 250 metres and take the first right onto a narrow, overgrown road. Parking lot is at end. A 10-minute hike through the forest on a marked trail brings you to the ocean. Walk south along the beach to reach the salt marsh and estuary.*

CLUXEWE SALT MARSH
Main Logging Road
Misty Main
Recycling Yard
To Port Hardy
P
BROUGHTON STRAIT
N
Cluxewe Salt Marsh
Campground
Hwy 19
Cluxewe R

*Male Bufflehead. Photo: Frank Stoney*

ly protected are subject to tremendous pressure and degradation from industrial and agricultural activity and from real estate development spurred by the demand for "water view" property. The Cluxewe salt marsh is protected through the combined efforts of The Nature Trust of British Columbia and a BC Environment Wildlife Reserve. The equally important estuary and intertidal foreshore are not currently protected.

Spending a night at the Broughton Strait Resort Campground 13 kilometres north of Port McNeill will place you right on the sandspit of the estuary, which is great for birdwatchers. But the large number of campers and dogs in the spring deters the Brant and other birds from fully using the spit. Otherwise, use the public access to the salt marsh and east bank. The salt marsh is shown on the Western Forest Products recreation map for Northern Vancouver Island, available from the Port McNeill tourist bureau.

*Mallards (male on right) are the most abundant dabbling duck on the estuary. Photo: Kim Goldberg*

**Port McNeill Tourist Information Centre:**        250-956-3131

*Full moon over Nanaimo estuary. Photo: Kim Goldberg*

# Vancouver Island Top 40

## Good places to look for the most popular species

❏ **American Bittern**  Buttertubs Marsh (64), Hamilton Swamp (74).

❏ **American Dipper**  Goldstream Provincial Park (44), Stamp Falls Provincial Park (76), Big Qualicum Hatchery (94).

❏ **American Kestrel**  East Sooke Regional Park (30), Nanaimo River Estuary (56), Nanoose Hill (72).

❏ **Bald Eagle**  East Sooke Regional Park (30), Active Pass (42), Goldstream Provincial Park (44), Nanaimo River Estuary (56), virtually every coastal site.

❏ **Bats**  Goldstream Provincial Park (44).

❏ **Black Bear**  Strathcona Provincial Park—Thelwood Creek (122), Sayward to Port McNeill Highway (132).

❏ **Black Oystercatcher**  Victoria Waterfront (28), Nanaimo Waterfront Promenade (28), Newcastle Island Provincial Marine Park (62), most rocky shorelines.

❏ **Black Scoter**  Whiffen Spit (32), Island View Beach Regional Park (38), Deep Bay & Baynes Sound (96).

❏ **Brant goose**  Rathtrevor Beach Provincial Park (90), Parksville/Qualicum Beach (92), Courtenay River Estuary (100), Cluxewe Salt Marsh & Estuary (138).

❏ **Cougar**  Green Mountain (54), Strathcona Provincial Park—Elk River Valley (120), Sayward to Port McNeill Highway (132).

❏ **Eurasian Wigeon**  Victoria Waterfront (28), J.V. Clyne Bird Sanctuary (78), Rathtrevor Beach Provincial Park (90), potentially among any flock of American Wigeon.

❏ **Golden Eagle**  East Sooke Regional Park (30), Green Mountain (54).

❏ **Gray Whale**  Botanical Beach Provincial Park (34), Broken Group Islands (80), Long Beach (82).

❏ **Gray Wolf**  Green Mountain (54), Strathcona Provincial Park—Elk River Valley (120) and Thelwood Creek (122), Sayward to Port McNeill Highway (132).

❏ **Great Blue Heron**  Swan Lake/Christmas Hill Nature Sanctuary (36), Buttertubs Marsh (64), Nanaimo Waterfront Promenade (28), most coastal sites and wetlands.

❏ **Green Heron**  Cowichan Estuary (48), Cowichan River Dyke Trail (50), Somenos Marsh (52).

❏ **Harlequin Duck**  Victoria Waterfront (28), Piper's Lagoon (70), Big Qualicum Hatchery (94), common in coastal waters and streams.

❏ **Killer Whale**  Active Pass (42), Discovery Passage & Cape Mudge (114), Ripple Rock Trail (126), Johnstone Strait & Blackfish Sound (134).

❏ **Marbled Murrelet**  Victoria Waterfront (28), Sidney Spit Provincial Marine Park (40), Oyster Bay (110), Discovery Passage & Cape Mudge (114), Alert Bay (136), most coastal ocean sites and ferry crossings.

❏ **Merlin**  Nanaimo River Estuary (56), Tofino Flats (86), Woodhus Slough (108).

- ❑ **Muskrat** Swan Lake/Christmas Hill Nature Sanctuary (36), Buttertubs Marsh (64), Woodhus Slough (108).
- ❑ **Northern Alligator Lizard** Nanoose Hill (72).
- ❑ **Northern Pygmy-owl** Goldstream Provincial Park (44).
- ❑ **Northern Shrike** Island View Beach Regional Park (38), Cowichan Estuary (48), Nanaimo River Estuary (56).
- ❑ **Osprey** Cowichan Estuary (48), Nanaimo River Estuary (56), Salmon River Estuary (130), near rivers, lakes and coastal shoreline.
- ❑ **Peregrine Falcon** East Sooke Regional Park (30), Martindale Flats en route to Island View Beach (38), Nanaimo River Estuary (56).
- ❑ **Pigeon Guillemot** Sidney Spit Provincial Marine Park (40), Northumberland Channel (58), Discovery Passage & Cape Mudge (114), Alert Bay (136), most coastal ocean sites and ferry crossings.
- ❑ **Pileated Woodpecker** Newcastle Island Provincial Marine Park (62), Rathtrevor Beach Provincial Park (90), Miracle Beach Provincial Park (106).
- ❑ **Purple Martin** Cowichan Estuary (48), Nanaimo River Estuary (56), Newcastle Island Provincial Marine Park (62).
- ❑ **Red-tailed Hawk** East Sooke Regional Park (30), Somenos Marsh (52), Buttertubs Marsh (64), Salmon River Estuary (130), common over farm fields and wetlands.
- ❑ **Rhinoceros Auklet** Victoria Waterfront (28), Island View Beach Regional Park (38), Mitlenatch Island Provincial Marine Park (112), coastal ocean sites and ferry crossings.
- ❑ **Roosevelt Elk** Green Mountain (54), Menzies Elk Demonstration Forest (124), Strathcona Provincial Park—Elk River Valley (120), Sayward to Port McNeill Highway (132).
- ❑ **Sea Lion** Northumberland Channel (58), Deep Bay & Baynes Sound (96), Lambert Channel en route to Helliwell Provincial Park (98).
- ❑ **Trumpeter Swan** Cowichan Estuary (48), Somenos Marsh (52), Nanaimo River Estuary (56), Courtenay River Estuary (100).
- ❑ **Tufted Puffin** Victoria Waterfront (28), Mandarte Island off Sidney Spit Provincial Marine Park (40), Cleland Island near Tofino (86).
- ❑ **Turkey Vulture** East Sooke Regional Park (30), seasonally common over fields and other open habitat.
- ❑ **Vancouver Island Marmot** Green Mountain (54).
- ❑ **Virginia Rail** Buttertubs Marsh (64), Woodhus Slough (108).
- ❑ **Western Grebe** Piper's Lagoon (70), Deep Bay & Baynes Sound (96), Oyster Bay (110).
- ❑ **Western Screech-owl** Miracle Beach Provincial Park (106), Alert Bay (136).

*The American Bittern is a master of disguise.*
*Photo: Rick Ikona*

# Checklist of Vancouver Island Mammals

## including adjacent islands and coastal waters

Common and Latin names and taxonomic sequence conform to the Royal British Columbia Museum publication *The Mammals of British Columbia: A Taxonomic Catalogue* by David Nagorsen.

Names in red were on the provincial government's Red List of indigenous species or Vancouver Island subspecies considered threatened or endangered or candidates for these designations in 1997. Names in blue were on the provincial government's Blue List of indigenous species or Vancouver Island subspecies considered vulnerable in 1997. Names in **bold** are introduced species. Subspecies is given only for mammals whose Vancouver Island subspecies is Red-listed or Blue-listed.

❑ **North American Opossum** (*Didelphis virginiana*; Hornby Island)
❑ Dusky Shrew (*Sorex monticulus*)
❑ Water Shrew (*Sorex palustris brooksi*)
❑ Vagrant Shrew (*Sorex vagrans*)
❑ Big Brown Bat (*Eptesicus fuscus*)
❑ Silver-haired Bat (*Lasionycteris noctivagans*)
❑ Hoary Bat (*Lasiurus cinereus*)
❑ California Myotis (*Myotis californicus*)
❑ Western Long-eared Myotis (*Myotis evotis*)
❑ Keen's Long-eared Myotis (*Myotis keenii*)
❑ Little Brown Myotis (*Myotis lucifugus*)
❑ Long-legged Myotis (*Myotis volans*)
❑ Yuma Myotis (*Myotis yumanensis*)
❑ Townsend's Big-eared Bat (*Plecotus townsendii*)
❑ **European Rabbit** (*Oryctolagus cuniculus*)
❑ **Eastern Cottontail** (*Sylvilagus floridanus*)
❑ Townsend's Vole (*Microtus townsendii*)
❑ **Muskrat** (*Ondatra zibethicus*)
❑ Beaver (*Castor canadensis*)
❑ Deer Mouse (*Peromyscus maniculatus*)
❑ Keen's Mouse (*Peromyscus keeni*)
❑ **House Mouse** (*Mus musculus*)
❑ **Norway Rat** (*Rattus norvegicus*)

- ❏ **Black Rat** (*Rattus rattus*)
- ❏ Northern Flying Squirrel (*Glaucomys sabrinus*; Quadra and Cortes islands)
- ❏ Vancouver Island Marmot (*Marmota vancouverensis*)
- ❏ **Gray Squirrel** (*Sciurus carolinensis*)
- ❏ Red Squirrel (*Tamiasciurus hudsonicus*)
- ❏ Gray Wolf (*Canis lupus*)
- ❏ Cougar (*Felix concolor*)
- ❏ Sea Otter (*Enhydra lutris*)
- ❏ Wolverine (*Gulo gulo vancouverensis*)
- ❏ River Otter (*Lontra canadensis*)
- ❏ Marten (*Martes americana*)
- ❏ Ermine (*Mustela erminea anguinae*)
- ❏ Mink (*Mustela vison*)
- ❏ Northern Fur Seal (*Callorhinus ursinus*)
- ❏ Northern Sea Lion (*Eumetopias jubatus*)
- ❏ California Sea Lion (*Zalophus californianus*)
- ❏ Northern Elephant Seal (*Mirounga angustirostris*)
- ❏ Harbor Seal (*Phoca vitulina*)
- ❏ Raccoon (*Procyon lotor*)
- ❏ Black Bear (*Ursus americanus*)
- ❏ Minke Whale (*Balaenoptera acutorostrata*)
- ❏ Humpback Whale (*Megaptera novaeangliae*)
- ❏ Pacific White-sided Dolphin (*Lagenorhynchus obliquidens*)
- ❏ Killer Whale (*Orcinus orca*)
- ❏ Gray Whale (*Eschrichtius robustus*)
- ❏ Harbor Porpoise (*Phocoena phocoena*)
- ❏ Dall's Porpoise (*Phocoenoides dalli*)
- ❏ **Fallow Deer** (*Cervus dama*; Sidney and James islands)
- ❏ Roosevelt Elk (*Cervus elaphus roosevelti*)
- ❏ Black-tailed Deer (*Odocoileus hemionus*)

Vancouver
Island Marmot.
Photo:
Trudy Chatwin

# Checklist of Vancouver Island Herptiles

Common and Latin names and taxonomic sequence conform to the Royal British Columbia Museum Handbooks *The Amphibians of British Columbia* by David M. Green and R. Wayne Campbell and *The Reptiles of British Columbia* by Patrick T. Gregory and R. Wayne Campbell.

Names in red were on the provincial government's Red List of indigenous species or Vancouver Island subspecies considered threatened or endangered, or candidates for these designations, in 1997. Names in blue were on the provincial government's Blue List of indigenous species or Vancouver Island subspecies considered vulnerable in 1997. Names in **bold** are introduced species or subspecies.

## AMPHIBIANS
### SALAMANDERS
❏ Rough-skinned Newt (*Taricha granulosa*)
❏ Long-toed Salamander (*Ambystoma macrodactylum*)
❏ Northwestern Salamander (*Ambystoma gracile*)
❏ Western Red-backed Salamander (*Plethodon vehiculum*)
❏ Ensatina (*Ensatina eschscholtzii*)
❏ Clouded Salamander (*Aneides ferreus*)

### FROGS & TOADS
❏ Western Toad (*Bufo boreas*)
❏ Pacific Treefrog (*Hyla regilla*)
❏ Red-legged Frog (*Rana aurora*)
❏ Northern Leopard Frog (*Rana pipiens*; not Red-listed on Vancouver Island, where it is introduced)
❏ **Bullfrog** (*Rana catesbeiana*)
❏ **Green Frog (***Rana clamitans***)**

## REPTILES
### TURTLES
❏ Painted Turtle (*Chrysemys picta*; not Blue-listed on Vancouver Island, where it is introduced)
❏ Pacific Green Turtle (*Chelonia mydas agassizi*; one record from Ucluelet)
❏ Pacific Leatherback (*Dermochelys coriacea schlegeli*)
❏ Western Skink (*Eumeces skiltonianus skiltonianus*; one sighting NW of Courtenay)
❏ Northern Alligator Lizard (*Elgaria coerulea principis*)

145

SNAKES
- ❏ Sharptail Snake (*Contia tenuis*)
- ❏ Pacific Gopher Snake (*Pituophis melanoleucus catenifer*; one specimen from Galiano Island)
- ❏ Puget Sound Garter Snake (*Thamnophis sirtalis pickeringi*; subspecies of Common Garter Snake)
- ❏ Northwestern Garter Snake (*Thamnophis ordinoides*)
- ❏ Wandering Garter Snake (*Thamnophis elegans vagrans*; BC subspecies of Western Terrestrial Garter Snake)

# Have You Seen This Snake?

*Photo: Alula Biological Consulting*

## Sharptail Snake

Sharptail Snake is one of BC's rarest native animals and is on the provincial government's Red List of Threatened or Endangered species. Most sightings are from southern Vancouver Island and the southern Gulf Islands. More information is needed about this snake's abundance and distribution in BC. If you see this small, harmless, brown snake—about the size of a large earthworm, with a divided anal plate, a thornlike tail tip and a barred belly—report it to the Wildlife Branch in Victoria at **250-387-9755**.

# Checklist of Vancouver Island Butterflies

Species shown in red type are extirpated from Vancouver Island

- ❑ Silver-spotted Skipper (*Epargyreus clarus*)
- ❑ Northern Cloudy Wing (*Thorybes pylades*)
- ❑ Dreamy Dusky Wing (*Erynnis icelus*)
- ❑ Propertius Dusky Wing (*Erynnis propertius*)
- ❑ Persius Dusky Wing (*Erynnis persius* spp. undetermined)
- ❑ Two-banded Checkered Skipper (*Pyrgus ruralis ruralis*)
- ❑ Arctic Skipper (*Carterocephalus palaemon mandan*)
- ❑ European Skipper (*Thymelicus lineola*)
- ❑ Common Branded Skipper (*Hesperia comma oregonia*)
- ❑ Woodland Skipper (*Ochlodes sylvanoides sylvanoides*)
- ❑ Dun Skipper (*Euphyes vestris metacomet*)
- ❑ Roadside Skipper (*Amblyscirtes vialis*)
- ❑ Clodius Parnassian (*Parnassius clodius claudianus*)
- ❑ Phoebus' Parnassian (*Parnassius phoebus olympianus*)
- ❑ Anise Swallowtail (*Papilio zelicaon zelicaon*)
- ❑ Western Tiger Swallowtail (*Papilio rutulus rutulus*)
- ❑ Pale Swallowtail (*Papilio eurymedon*)
- ❑ Pine White (*Neophasia menapia tau*)
- ❑ Western White (*Pontia occidentalis occidentalis*)
- ❑ Mustard White (*Pieris napi marginalis*)
- ❑ Cabbage Butterfly (*Pieris rapae*)
- ❑ Large Marble (*Euchloe ausonides* spp. undescribed)
- ❑ Sara Orange Tip (*Anthocharis sara flora*)
- ❑ Clouded Sulphur (*Colias philodice eriphyle*)
- ❑ Alfalfa Butterfly (*Colias eurytheme*)
- ❑ Western Sulphur (*Colias occidentalis occidentalis*)
- ❑ Purplish Copper (*Epidemia helloides*)
- ❑ Reakirt's Copper (*Epidemia mariposa charlottensis & penroseae*)
- ❑ Acadian Hairstreak (*Satyrium acadicum*)
- ❑ Johnson's Hairstreak (*Mitoura johnsoni*)
- ❑ Rosner's Hairstreak (*Mitoura rosneri plicataria*)
- ❑ Barry's Hairstreak (*Mitoura barryi acuminata*)
- ❑ Brown Elfin (*Incisalia augustinus iroides*)
- ❑ Moss' Elfin (*Incisalia mossi mossi*)
- ❑ Western Pine Elfin (*Incisalia eryphon sheltonensis*)
- ❑ Gray Hairstreak (*Strymon melinus atrofasciatus*)
- ❑ Western Tailed Blue (*Everes amyntula albrighti*)
- ❑ Spring Azure (*Celastrina argiolus echo*)

❏ Silvery Blue (*Glaucopsyche lygdamus columbia*)
❏ Northern Blue (*Lycaeides idas* spp. undetermined)
❏ Greenish Blue (*Plebejus saepiolus insulanus*)
❏ Icarioides Blue (*Icaricia icarioides blackmorei*)
❏ Rustic Blue (*Agriades rusticus megalo*)
❏ Zerene Fritillary (*Speyeria zerene bremneri*)
❏ Hydaspe Fritillary (*Speyeria hydaspe rhodope*)
❏ Western Meadow Fritillary (*Clossiana epithore uslui*)
❏ Field Crescent (*Phyciodes pratensis pratensis*)
❏ Mylitta Crescent (*Phyciodes mylitta mylitta*)
❏ Chalcedon Checkerspot (*Euphydryas chalcedona perdiccas*)
❏ Edith's Checkerspot (*Euphydryas editha taylori*)
❏ Satyr Anglewing (*Polygonia satyrus*)
❏ Green Comma (*Polygonia faunus rusticus*)
❏ Zephyr Anglewing (*Polygonia zephyrus*)
❏ Oreas Anglewing (*Polygonia oreas silenus*)
❏ California Tortoise Shell (*Nymphalis californica*)
❏ Mourning Cloak (*Nymphalis antiopa antiopa*)
❏ Milbert's Tortoise Shell (*Nymphalis milberti milberti*)
❏ American Painted Lady (*Vanessa virginiensis*)
❏ Painted Lady (*Vanessa cardui*)
❏ West Coast Lady (*Vanessa annabella*)
❏ Red Admiral (*Vanessa atalanta rubria*)
❏ Lorquin's Admiral (*Basilarchia lorquini burrisoni*)
❏ Ringlet (*Coenonympha tullia insulana*)
❏ Common Wood Nymph (*Cercyonis pegala incana*)
❏ Great Arctic (*Oeneis nevadensis gigas*)
❏ Monarch (*Danaus plexippus*)

*Checklist supplied by Cris Guppy*

*Western Tiger Swallowtail. Photo: Lothar Kirchner*

## SEASONAL ABUNDANCE OF SELECTED BUTTERFILES
## OF SOUTHERN VANCOUVER ISLAND

| | | | |
|---|---|---|---|
| ■ | Hard to miss | W-R | Between widespread and restricted |
| ■ | Should see | R | Restricted to specific habitats |
| ▬ | May see | L | Highly localized (in 1-6 locations only) |
| — | Slight possibility | M | Migratory |
| --- | How lucky can you get? | Ac | Accidental |
| ↦ | 1 record only—arrow indicates | H | Hibernates |
| | how long it was seen | U | Uncertain status |
| ? | Unconfirmed sighting | D | Declining |
| W | Widespread | | |

*Bar graph supplied by Steve Ansell*

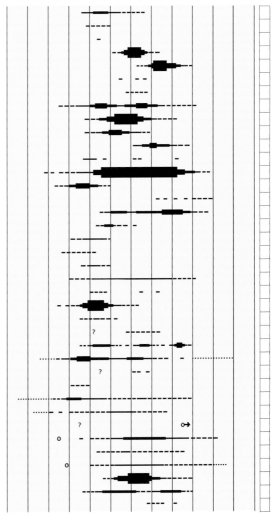

| | |
|---|---|
| Propertius Dusky Wing | R |
| Two-Banded Checkered Skipper | L |
| Arctic Skipper (U) | L |
| European Skipper | R |
| Woodland Skipper | W |
| Dun Skipper | L |
| Clodius Parnassian | R |
| Anise Swallowtail | W |
| Western Tiger Swallowtail | W |
| Pale Swallowtail | W-R |
| Pine White | W-R |
| Mustard White (U) | R |
| Cabbage Butterfly | W |
| Sara Orange Tip | W-R |
| Alfalfa Butterfly | L |
| Purplish Copper | W |
| Rosner's Hairstreak | L |
| Brown Elfin | R |
| Moss' Elfin | L |
| Western Pine Elfin | L |
| Gray Hairstreak | W |
| Western Tailed Blue (D) | L |
| Spring Azure | W |
| Silvery Blue (D) | L |
| Hydaspe Fritillary | R |
| Mylitta Crescent | W |
| Satyr Anglewing | W/H |
| Green Comma (U) | R |
| California Tortoise Shell | M |
| Mourning Cloak | W/H |
| Milbert's Tortoise Shell | W/H |
| American Painted Lady | Ac |
| Painted Lady | W/M |
| West Coast Lady | W |
| Red Admiral | W |
| Lorquin's Admiral | W |
| Ringlet | R |
| Common Wood Nymph (U) | L |

Brown Elfin.
Photo: Ian Lane

Rosner's Hairstreak.
Photo: Richard Beard

Western Pine Elfin.
Photo: Ian Lane

Plain Ringlet.
Photo: Ian Lane

Gray Hairstreak.
Photo: Ian Lane

Spring Azure, female.
Photo: Lothar Kirchner

Cabbage Butterfly.
*Photo: Lothar Kirchner*

Pine White, female.
*Photo: Ian Lane*

Mustard White.
*Photo: Cris Guppy*

Lorquin's Admiral.
*Photo: Richard Beard*

Purplish Copper, male.
*Photo: Lothar Kirchner*

Painted Lady.
*Photo: Lothar Kirchner*

West Coast Lady.
*Photo: Lothar Kirchner*

Milbert's Tortoiseshell.
Photo: Lothar Kirchner

Satyr Comma.
Photo: Cris Guppy

Mourning Cloak.
Photo: Lothar Kirchner

Anise Swallowtail.
Photo: Lothar Kirchner

Silvery Blue.
Photo: Lothar Kirchner

Edith's Checkerspot.
Photo: Lothar Kirchner

Western Meadow Fritillary.
Photo: Lothar Kirchner

# Checklist of Vancouver Island Birds

*Supplied by Keith Taylor*

The following symbols depict the probability of an individual to see at least one bird in appropriate habitat at the correct season.

██████ Hard to miss

████ Should see

──── May see

············ How lucky can you get

• Vagrant—not recorded annually

o Accidental—fewer than 10 records for the province

. Rare—recorded annually in low numbers

SYMBOLS

* Nesting—one successful breeding record

[A] Accidental

[R] Rare

[H] Hypothetical—well-documented but requires photograph

[H*] Hypothetical—waiting acceptance by records commitee

[SR] Sight record—written descriptions by few observers

? Questionable record—not well-documented

[I] Introduced—successfully established for 10 years plus

[NC] Not countable—introduced species not established

[X] e Extirpated—species that has vanished in modern times

[L] Local—populations confined to localized sites

[origin?] Possible aviary escapee

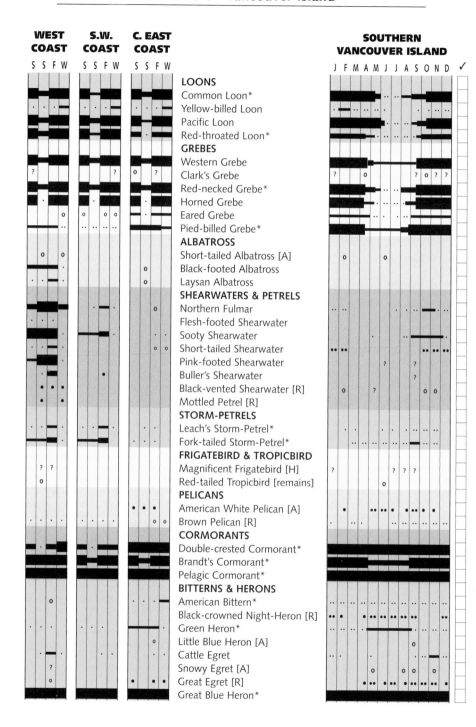

| WEST COAST | S.W. COAST | C. EAST COAST | | SOUTHERN VANCOUVER ISLAND |
|---|---|---|---|---|
| S S F W | S S F W | S S F W | | J F M A M J J A S O N D ✓ |

**LOONS**
Common Loon*
Yellow-billed Loon
Pacific Loon
Red-throated Loon*
**GREBES**
Western Grebe
Clark's Grebe
Red-necked Grebe*
Horned Grebe
Eared Grebe
Pied-billed Grebe*
**ALBATROSS**
Short-tailed Albatross [A]
Black-footed Albatross
Laysan Albatross
**SHEARWATERS & PETRELS**
Northern Fulmar
Flesh-footed Shearwater
Sooty Shearwater
Short-tailed Shearwater
Pink-footed Shearwater
Buller's Shearwater
Black-vented Shearwater [R]
Mottled Petrel [R]
**STORM-PETRELS**
Leach's Storm-Petrel*
Fork-tailed Storm-Petrel*
**FRIGATEBIRD & TROPICBIRD**
Magnificent Frigatebird [H]
Red-tailed Tropicbird [remains]
**PELICANS**
American White Pelican [A]
Brown Pelican [R]
**CORMORANTS**
Double-crested Cormorant*
Brandt's Cormorant*
Pelagic Cormorant*
**BITTERNS & HERONS**
American Bittern*
Black-crowned Night-Heron [R]
Green Heron*
Little Blue Heron [A]
Cattle Egret
Snowy Egret [A]
Great Egret [R]
Great Blue Heron*

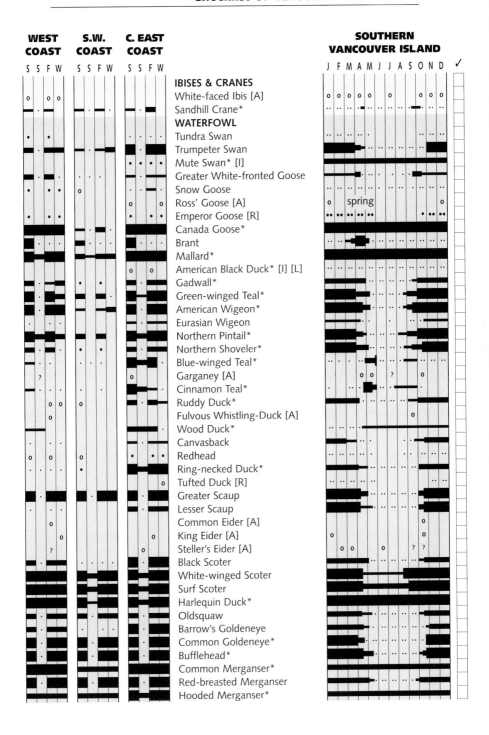

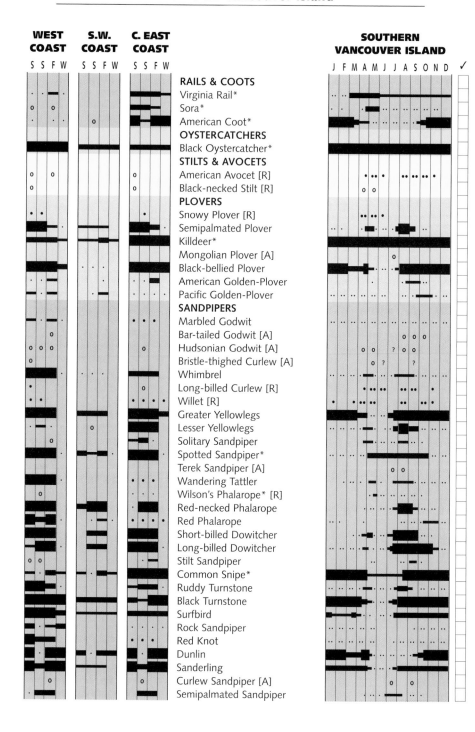

| WEST COAST | S.W. COAST | C. EAST COAST | | SOUTHERN VANCOUVER ISLAND | |
|---|---|---|---|---|---|
| S S F W | S S F W | S S F W | | J F M A M J J A S O N D | ✓ |

RAILS & COOTS
Virginia Rail*
Sora*
American Coot*
OYSTERCATCHERS
Black Oystercatcher*
STILTS & AVOCETS
American Avocet [R]
Black-necked Stilt [R]
PLOVERS
Snowy Plover [R]
Semipalmated Plover
Killdeer*
Mongolian Plover [A]
Black-bellied Plover
American Golden-Plover
Pacific Golden-Plover
SANDPIPERS
Marbled Godwit
Bar-tailed Godwit [A]
Hudsonian Godwit [A]
Bristle-thighed Curlew [A]
Whimbrel
Long-billed Curlew [R]
Willet [R]
Greater Yellowlegs
Lesser Yellowlegs
Solitary Sandpiper
Spotted Sandpiper*
Terek Sandpiper [A]
Wandering Tattler
Wilson's Phalarope* [R]
Red-necked Phalarope
Red Phalarope
Short-billed Dowitcher
Long-billed Dowitcher
Stilt Sandpiper
Common Snipe*
Ruddy Turnstone
Black Turnstone
Surfbird
Rock Sandpiper
Red Knot
Dunlin
Sanderling
Curlew Sandpiper [A]
Semipalmated Sandpiper

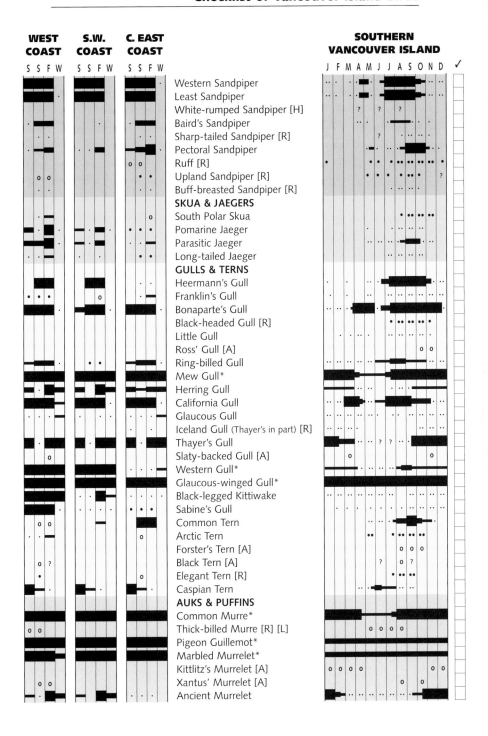

| WEST COAST | S.W. COAST | C. EAST COAST | | SOUTHERN VANCOUVER ISLAND | ✓ |
|---|---|---|---|---|---|
| S S F W | S S F W | S S F W | | J F M A M J J A S O N D | |
| | | | Western Sandpiper | | |
| | | | Least Sandpiper | | |
| | | | White-rumped Sandpiper [H] | | |
| | | | Baird's Sandpiper | | |
| | | | Sharp-tailed Sandpiper [R] | | |
| | | | Pectoral Sandpiper | | |
| | | | Ruff [R] | | |
| | | | Upland Sandpiper [R] | | |
| | | | Buff-breasted Sandpiper [R] | | |
| | | | **SKUA & JAEGERS** | | |
| | | | South Polar Skua | | |
| | | | Pomarine Jaeger | | |
| | | | Parasitic Jaeger | | |
| | | | Long-tailed Jaeger | | |
| | | | **GULLS & TERNS** | | |
| | | | Heermann's Gull | | |
| | | | Franklin's Gull | | |
| | | | Bonaparte's Gull | | |
| | | | Black-headed Gull [R] | | |
| | | | Little Gull | | |
| | | | Ross' Gull [A] | | |
| | | | Ring-billed Gull | | |
| | | | Mew Gull* | | |
| | | | Herring Gull | | |
| | | | California Gull | | |
| | | | Glaucous Gull | | |
| | | | Iceland Gull (Thayer's in part) [R] | | |
| | | | Thayer's Gull | | |
| | | | Slaty-backed Gull [A] | | |
| | | | Western Gull* | | |
| | | | Glaucous-winged Gull* | | |
| | | | Black-legged Kittiwake | | |
| | | | Sabine's Gull | | |
| | | | Common Tern | | |
| | | | Arctic Tern | | |
| | | | Forster's Tern [A] | | |
| | | | Black Tern [A] | | |
| | | | Elegant Tern [R] | | |
| | | | Caspian Tern | | |
| | | | **AUKS & PUFFINS** | | |
| | | | Common Murre* | | |
| | | | Thick-billed Murre [R] [L] | | |
| | | | Pigeon Guillemot* | | |
| | | | Marbled Murrelet* | | |
| | | | Kittlitz's Murrelet [A] | | |
| | | | Xantus' Murrelet [A] | | |
| | | | Ancient Murrelet | | |

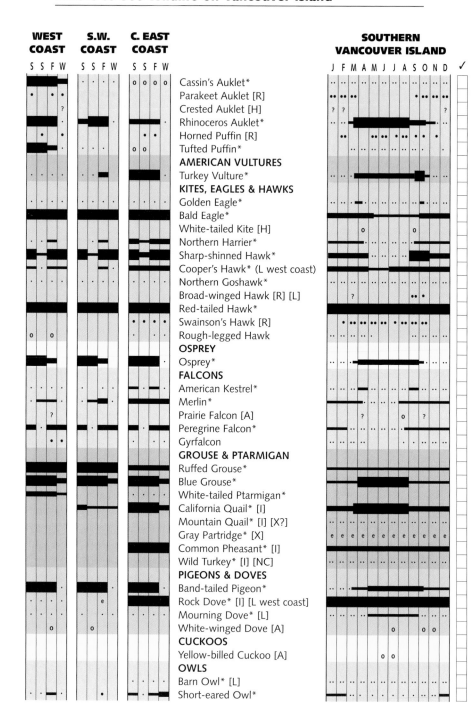

| WEST COAST | S.W. COAST | C. EAST COAST | | SOUTHERN VANCOUVER ISLAND |
|---|---|---|---|---|
| S S F W | S S F W | S S F W | | J F M A M J J A S O N D ✓ |

Cassin's Auklet*
Parakeet Auklet [R]
Crested Auklet [H]
Rhinoceros Auklet*
Horned Puffin [R]
Tufted Puffin*

**AMERICAN VULTURES**
Turkey Vulture*

**KITES, EAGLES & HAWKS**
Golden Eagle*
Bald Eagle*
White-tailed Kite [H]
Northern Harrier*
Sharp-shinned Hawk*
Cooper's Hawk* (L west coast)
Northern Goshawk*
Broad-winged Hawk [R] [L]
Red-tailed Hawk*
Swainson's Hawk [R]
Rough-legged Hawk

**OSPREY**
Osprey*

**FALCONS**
American Kestrel*
Merlin*
Prairie Falcon [A]
Peregrine Falcon*
Gyrfalcon

**GROUSE & PTARMIGAN**
Ruffed Grouse*
Blue Grouse*
White-tailed Ptarmigan*
California Quail* [I]
Mountain Quail* [I] [X?]
Gray Partridge* [X]
Common Pheasant* [I]
Wild Turkey* [I] [NC]

**PIGEONS & DOVES**
Band-tailed Pigeon*
Rock Dove* [I] [L west coast]
Mourning Dove* [L]
White-winged Dove [A]

**CUCKOOS**
Yellow-billed Cuckoo [A]

**OWLS**
Barn Owl* [L]
Short-eared Owl*

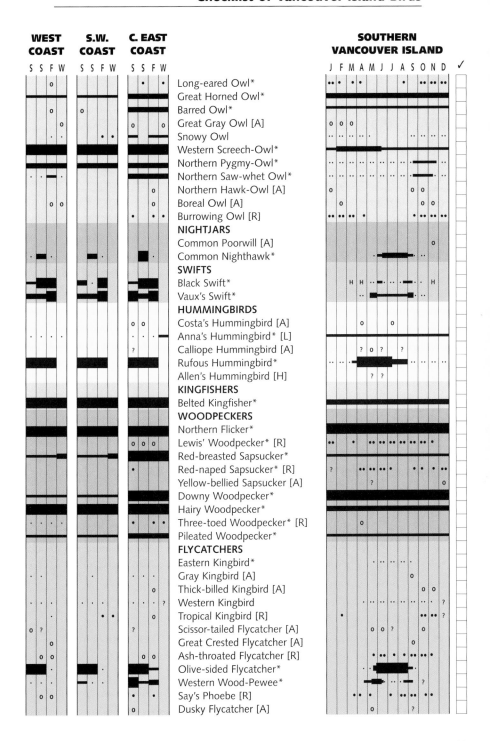

| WEST COAST | S.W. COAST | C. EAST COAST | | SOUTHERN VANCOUVER ISLAND | |
|---|---|---|---|---|---|
| S S F W | S S F W | S S F W | | J F M A M J J A S O N D | ✓ |

Long-eared Owl*
Great Horned Owl*
Barred Owl*
Great Gray Owl [A]
Snowy Owl
Western Screech-Owl*
Northern Pygmy-Owl*
Northern Saw-whet Owl*
Northern Hawk-Owl [A]
Boreal Owl [A]
Burrowing Owl [R]
**NIGHTJARS**
Common Poorwill [A]
Common Nighthawk*
**SWIFTS**
Black Swift*
Vaux's Swift*
**HUMMINGBIRDS**
Costa's Hummingbird [A]
Anna's Hummingbird* [L]
Calliope Hummingbird [A]
Rufous Hummingbird*
Allen's Hummingbird [H]
**KINGFISHERS**
Belted Kingfisher*
**WOODPECKERS**
Northern Flicker*
Lewis' Woodpecker* [R]
Red-breasted Sapsucker*
Red-naped Sapsucker* [R]
Yellow-bellied Sapsucker [A]
Downy Woodpecker*
Hairy Woodpecker*
Three-toed Woodpecker* [R]
Pileated Woodpecker*
**FLYCATCHERS**
Eastern Kingbird*
Gray Kingbird [A]
Thick-billed Kingbird [A]
Western Kingbird
Tropical Kingbird [R]
Scissor-tailed Flycatcher [A]
Great Crested Flycatcher [A]
Ash-throated Flycatcher [R]
Olive-sided Flycatcher*
Western Wood-Pewee*
Say's Phoebe [R]
Dusky Flycatcher [A]

159

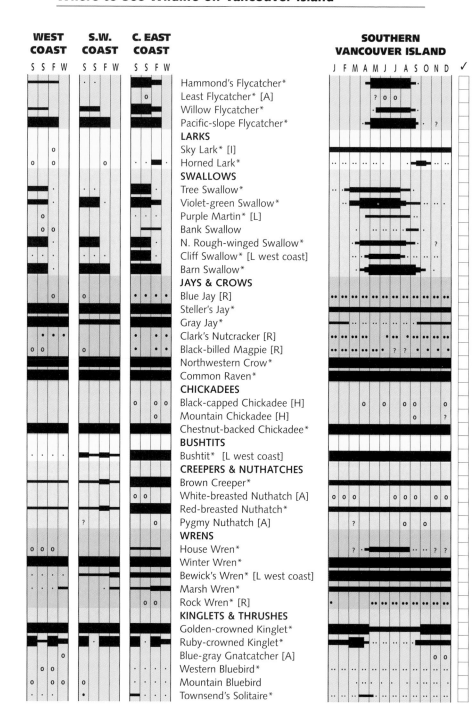

| WEST COAST | S.W. COAST | C. EAST COAST | | SOUTHERN VANCOUVER ISLAND |
| --- | --- | --- | --- | --- |
| S S F W | S S F W | S S F W | | J F M A M J J A S O N D ✓ |

Hammond's Flycatcher*
Least Flycatcher* [A]
Willow Flycatcher*
Pacific-slope Flycatcher*
**LARKS**
Sky Lark* [I]
Horned Lark*
**SWALLOWS**
Tree Swallow*
Violet-green Swallow*
Purple Martin* [L]
Bank Swallow
N. Rough-winged Swallow*
Cliff Swallow* [L west coast]
Barn Swallow*
**JAYS & CROWS**
Blue Jay [R]
Steller's Jay*
Gray Jay*
Clark's Nutcracker [R]
Black-billed Magpie [R]
Northwestern Crow*
Common Raven*
**CHICKADEES**
Black-capped Chickadee [H]
Mountain Chickadee [H]
Chestnut-backed Chickadee*
**BUSHTITS**
Bushtit* [L west coast]
**CREEPERS & NUTHATCHES**
Brown Creeper*
White-breasted Nuthatch [A]
Red-breasted Nuthatch*
Pygmy Nuthatch [A]
**WRENS**
House Wren*
Winter Wren*
Bewick's Wren* [L west coast]
Marsh Wren*
Rock Wren* [R]
**KINGLETS & THRUSHES**
Golden-crowned Kinglet*
Ruby-crowned Kinglet*
Blue-gray Gnatcatcher [A]
Western Bluebird*
Mountain Bluebird
Townsend's Solitaire*

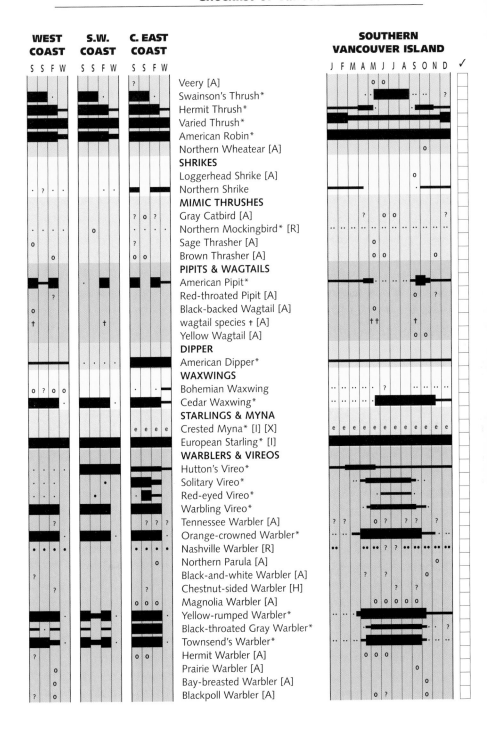

| WEST COAST | S.W. COAST | C. EAST COAST | | SOUTHERN VANCOUVER ISLAND |
|---|---|---|---|---|
| S S F W | S S F W | S S F W | | J F M A M J J A S O N D ✓ |

Veery [A]
Swainson's Thrush*
Hermit Thrush*
Varied Thrush*
American Robin*
Northern Wheatear [A]

**SHRIKES**
Loggerhead Shrike [A]
Northern Shrike

**MIMIC THRUSHES**
Gray Catbird [A]
Northern Mockingbird* [R]
Sage Thrasher [A]
Brown Thrasher [A]

**PIPITS & WAGTAILS**
American Pipit*
Red-throated Pipit [A]
Black-backed Wagtail [A]
wagtail species † [A]
Yellow Wagtail [A]

**DIPPER**
American Dipper*

**WAXWINGS**
Bohemian Waxwing
Cedar Waxwing*

**STARLINGS & MYNA**
Crested Myna* [I] [X]
European Starling* [I]

**WARBLERS & VIREOS**
Hutton's Vireo*
Solitary Vireo*
Red-eyed Vireo*
Warbling Vireo*
Tennessee Warbler [A]
Orange-crowned Warbler*
Nashville Warbler [R]
Northern Parula [A]
Black-and-white Warbler [A]
Chestnut-sided Warbler [H]
Magnolia Warbler [A]
Yellow-rumped Warbler*
Black-throated Gray Warbler*
Townsend's Warbler*
Hermit Warbler [A]
Prairie Warbler [A]
Bay-breasted Warbler [A]
Blackpoll Warbler [A]

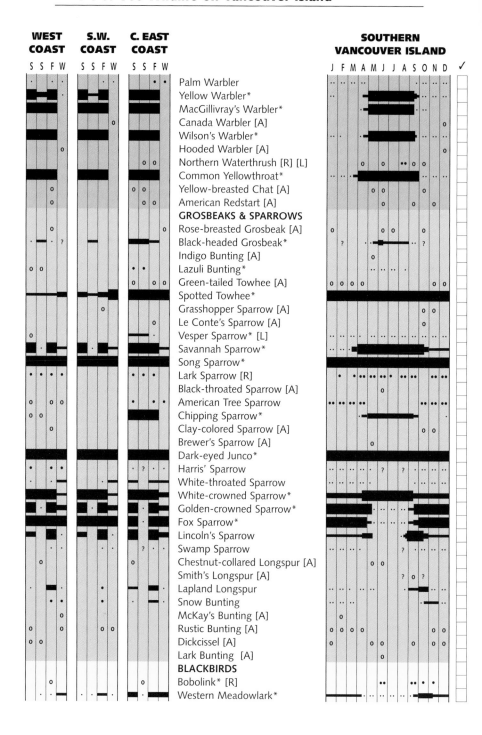

| | WEST COAST | | | | S.W. COAST | | | | C. EAST COAST | | | | | | SOUTHERN VANCOUVER ISLAND | | | | | | | | | | | | ✓ |
|---|---|---|---|---|---|---|---|---|---|---|---|---|---|---|---|---|---|---|---|---|---|---|---|---|---|---|---|---|
| | S | S | F | W | S | S | F | W | S | S | F | W | | | J | F | M | A | M | J | J | A | S | O | N | D | |
| Palm Warbler | | | | | | | | | | | | | | | | | | | | | | | | | | | |
| Yellow Warbler* | | | | | | | | | | | | | | | | | | | | | | | | | | | |
| MacGillivray's Warbler* | | | | | | | | | | | | | | | | | | | | | | | | | | | |
| Canada Warbler [A] | | | | | | | | | | | | | | | | | | | | | | | | | | | |
| Wilson's Warbler* | | | | | | | | | | | | | | | | | | | | | | | | | | | |
| Hooded Warbler [A] | | | | | | | | | | | | | | | | | | | | | | | | | | | |
| Northern Waterthrush [R] [L] | | | | | | | | | | | | | | | | | | | | | | | | | | | |
| Common Yellowthroat* | | | | | | | | | | | | | | | | | | | | | | | | | | | |
| Yellow-breasted Chat [A] | | | | | | | | | | | | | | | | | | | | | | | | | | | |
| American Redstart [A] | | | | | | | | | | | | | | | | | | | | | | | | | | | |
| **GROSBEAKS & SPARROWS** | | | | | | | | | | | | | | | | | | | | | | | | | | | |
| Rose-breasted Grosbeak [A] | | | | | | | | | | | | | | | | | | | | | | | | | | | |
| Black-headed Grosbeak* | | | | | | | | | | | | | | | | | | | | | | | | | | | |
| Indigo Bunting [A] | | | | | | | | | | | | | | | | | | | | | | | | | | | |
| Lazuli Bunting* | | | | | | | | | | | | | | | | | | | | | | | | | | | |
| Green-tailed Towhee [A] | | | | | | | | | | | | | | | | | | | | | | | | | | | |
| Spotted Towhee* | | | | | | | | | | | | | | | | | | | | | | | | | | | |
| Grasshopper Sparrow [A] | | | | | | | | | | | | | | | | | | | | | | | | | | | |
| Le Conte's Sparrow [A] | | | | | | | | | | | | | | | | | | | | | | | | | | | |
| Vesper Sparrow* [L] | | | | | | | | | | | | | | | | | | | | | | | | | | | |
| Savannah Sparrow* | | | | | | | | | | | | | | | | | | | | | | | | | | | |
| Song Sparrow* | | | | | | | | | | | | | | | | | | | | | | | | | | | |
| Lark Sparrow [R] | | | | | | | | | | | | | | | | | | | | | | | | | | | |
| Black-throated Sparrow [A] | | | | | | | | | | | | | | | | | | | | | | | | | | | |
| American Tree Sparrow | | | | | | | | | | | | | | | | | | | | | | | | | | | |
| Chipping Sparrow* | | | | | | | | | | | | | | | | | | | | | | | | | | | |
| Clay-colored Sparrow [A] | | | | | | | | | | | | | | | | | | | | | | | | | | | |
| Brewer's Sparrow [A] | | | | | | | | | | | | | | | | | | | | | | | | | | | |
| Dark-eyed Junco* | | | | | | | | | | | | | | | | | | | | | | | | | | | |
| Harris' Sparrow | | | | | | | | | | | | | | | | | | | | | | | | | | | |
| White-throated Sparrow | | | | | | | | | | | | | | | | | | | | | | | | | | | |
| White-crowned Sparrow* | | | | | | | | | | | | | | | | | | | | | | | | | | | |
| Golden-crowned Sparrow* | | | | | | | | | | | | | | | | | | | | | | | | | | | |
| Fox Sparrow* | | | | | | | | | | | | | | | | | | | | | | | | | | | |
| Lincoln's Sparrow | | | | | | | | | | | | | | | | | | | | | | | | | | | |
| Swamp Sparrow | | | | | | | | | | | | | | | | | | | | | | | | | | | |
| Chestnut-collared Longspur [A] | | | | | | | | | | | | | | | | | | | | | | | | | | | |
| Smith's Longspur [A] | | | | | | | | | | | | | | | | | | | | | | | | | | | |
| Lapland Longspur | | | | | | | | | | | | | | | | | | | | | | | | | | | |
| Snow Bunting | | | | | | | | | | | | | | | | | | | | | | | | | | | |
| McKay's Bunting [A] | | | | | | | | | | | | | | | | | | | | | | | | | | | |
| Rustic Bunting [A] | | | | | | | | | | | | | | | | | | | | | | | | | | | |
| Dickcissel [A] | | | | | | | | | | | | | | | | | | | | | | | | | | | |
| Lark Bunting [A] | | | | | | | | | | | | | | | | | | | | | | | | | | | |
| **BLACKBIRDS** | | | | | | | | | | | | | | | | | | | | | | | | | | | |
| Bobolink* [R] | | | | | | | | | | | | | | | | | | | | | | | | | | | |
| Western Meadowlark* | | | | | | | | | | | | | | | | | | | | | | | | | | | |

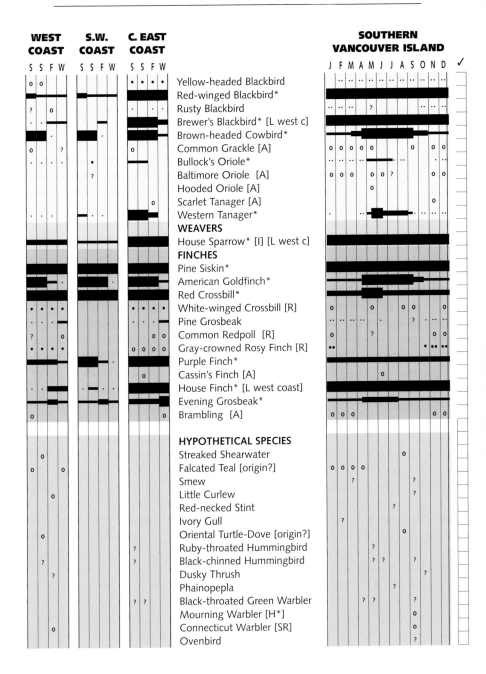

| WEST COAST | S.W. COAST | C. EAST COAST | | SOUTHERN VANCOUVER ISLAND |
|---|---|---|---|---|

Yellow-headed Blackbird
Red-winged Blackbird*
Rusty Blackbird
Brewer's Blackbird* [L west c]
Brown-headed Cowbird*
Common Grackle [A]
Bullock's Oriole*
Baltimore Oriole [A]
Hooded Oriole [A]
Scarlet Tanager [A]
Western Tanager*

**WEAVERS**
House Sparrow* [I] [L west c]

**FINCHES**
Pine Siskin*
American Goldfinch*
Red Crossbill*
White-winged Crossbill [R]
Pine Grosbeak
Common Redpoll [R]
Gray-crowned Rosy Finch [R]
Purple Finch*
Cassin's Finch [A]
House Finch* [L west coast]
Evening Grosbeak*
Brambling [A]

**HYPOTHETICAL SPECIES**
Streaked Shearwater
Falcated Teal [origin?]
Smew
Little Curlew
Red-necked Stint
Ivory Gull
Oriental Turtle-Dove [origin?]
Ruby-throated Hummingbird
Black-chinned Hummingbird
Dusky Thrush
Phainopepla
Black-throated Green Warbler
Mourning Warbler [H*]
Connecticut Warbler [SR]
Ovenbird

# Further Reading

If this book has aroused your curiosity about the fascinating animals, plants and natural history of Vancouver Island, then I urge you to look for and use any of the following excellent books for more detailed information. Each was extremely useful to me in preparing this book, and I sincerely thank their authors for taking the time to write them, thereby making the rest of us a little wiser and more appreciative of nature's wonders in this corner of the world.

Campbell, Eileen C., R. Wayne Campbell and Ronald T. McLaughlin. N.d. *Waterbirds of the Strait of Georgia*. MacMillan Bloedel Limited and British Columbia Waterfowl Society, Vancouver BC.

Campbell, R. Wayne, Neil K. Dawe, et al. 1990. *The Birds of British Columbia*, Vols. I and II. Royal British Columbia Museum, Victoria BC.

Corkran, Charlotte and Chris Thoms. 1996. *Amphibians of Oregon, Washington and British Columbia: A Field Identification Guide*. Lone Pine Publishing, Edmonton AB.

Green, David M. and R. Wayne Campbell. 1984. *The Amphibians of British Columbia*. Royal British Columbia Museum Handbook No. 45. Queen's Printer, Victoria BC.

Gregory, Patrick T. and R. Wayne Campbell. 1984. *The Reptiles of British Columbia*. Royal British Columbia Museum Handbook. Queen's Printer, Victoria BC.

Kozloff, Eugene N. 1976. *Plants and Animals of the Pacific Northwest*. Greystone Books, Douglas & McIntyre, Vancouver BC.

Lamb, Andy and Phil Edgell. 1986. *Coastal Fishes of the Pacific Northwest*. Harbour Publishing, Madeira Park BC.

McKenny, Margaret and Daniel E. Stuntz. 1994. *The New Savory Wild Mushroom*. Greystone Books, Douglas & McIntyre, Vancouver BC.

Nagorsen, David. 1990. *The Mammals of British Columbia: A Taxonomic Catalogue*. Royal British Columbia Museum Memoir No. 4. Queen's Printer, Victoria BC.

Nagorsen, David W. and R. Mark Brigham. 1993. *Bats of British Columbia*. Royal British Columbia Museum Handbook. UBC Press, Vancouver BC.

Paquet, Maggie M. 1990. *Parks of British Columbia and the Yukon*. Maia Publishing Limited, North Vancouver BC.

Pojar, Jim and Andy MacKinnon, eds. 1994. *Plants of Coastal British Columbia*. BC Ministry of Forests and Lone Pine Publishing, Victoria BC and Edmonton AB.

Snively, Gloria. 1978. *Exploring the Seashore in British Columbia, Washington and Oregon*. Gordon Soules, Vancouver BC.

Taylor, Keith. 1994. *Birder's Guide to Vancouver Island*. Keith Taylor Birdfinding Guides, Victoria BC.

Weston, Jim and David Stirling, eds. 1986. *The Naturalist's Guide to the Victoria Region*. Victoria Natural History Society, Victoria BC.

# Index

*Page numbers in bold indicate photographs.*